ROCK-A-BYE QUILTS

Babies and quilts— what a wonderful combination of new life and old tradition! In this timeless collection compiled from popular Leisure Arts publications, you'll find 10 quilted projects designed with baby's favorite things in mind. Cuddly bear cubs snooze among hearts on our matching quilt and wall hanging, while toy trains make their way around a blanket and coordinating bumper pads. There are other adorable accessories, as well, including a pretty springtime set adorned with hearts and flowers and a colorful ensemble featuring motifs from the popular nursery rhyme **Hey Diddle, Diddle.** *Updated with easy appliqués and time-saving techniques, the age-old craft of quilting is a perfect way to welcome brand-new bundles of joy!*

TABLE OF CONTENTS

NURSERY RHYME

CRIB QUILT

BLOCK SIZE: 7 1/2" x 7 1/2"
QUILT SIZE: 38" x 49"

YARDAGE REQUIREMENTS

Yardage is based on 45"w fabric.

- 1 1/2 yds of white print
- 7/8 yd of blue check
- 5/8 yd of gold check
- 3/8 yd of blue dot
- 3/8 yd of purple check
- 3/8 yd of purple stripe
- 1/8 yd of pink check
- 2 5/8 yds for backing
- 3/4 yd for binding
- 45" x 60" batting

You will also need:

paper-backed fusible web
transparent monofilament thread for appliqué

CUTTING OUT THE PIECES

*All measurements include seam allowances. Follow **Rotary Cutting**, page 41, to cut fabric.*

1. **From white print:**
   - Cut 4 **rectangles** 11" x 15" for triangle-squares.
   - Cut 2 **panels** 9" x 31 1/2".
2. **From blue check:**
   - Cut 2 **side outer borders** 3 1/2" x 41".
   - Cut 2 **top/bottom outer borders** 3 1/2" x 30 1/2".
   - Cut 1 **rectangle** 11" x 15" for triangle-squares.
3. **From gold check:**
   - Cut 2 **side inner borders** 1 1/4" x 41".
   - Cut 2 **top/bottom inner borders** 1 1/4" x 38".
   - Cut 4 **sashing strips** 1 1/4" x 30 1/2".
   - Cut 4 **sashing pieces** 1 1/4" x 3 1/2".
4. **From blue dot:**
   - Cut 1 **rectangle** 11" x 15" for triangle-squares.
5. **From purple check:**
   - Cut 1 **rectangle** 11" x 15" for triangle-squares.
6. **From purple stripe:**
   - Cut 1 **rectangle** 11" x 15" for triangle-squares.
7. **From pink check:**
   - Cut 4 **corner squares** 3 1/2" x 3 1/2".

PREPARING THE APPLIQUÉS

*Follow **Preparing Fusible Appliqués**, page 45, to cut appliqués using patterns, page 9.*

1. **From purple check:**
   - Cut 6 **bodies**.
2. **From pink check:**
   - Cut 6 **tails**.
   - Cut 6 **udders**.
   - Cut 6 **noses**.
   - Cut 12 **ears** (6 in reverse).
3. **From blue dot:**
   - Cut 6 **heads**.
4. **From gold check:**
   - Cut 12 **circles**.
   - Cut 4 **moons**.
   - Cut 14 **small stars**.

ASSEMBLING THE QUILT TOP

*Follow **Piecing and Pressing**, page 43, to make quilt top.*

1. To make triangle-squares, place 1 white print and blue check **rectangle** right sides together. Referring to **Fig. 1**, follow **Making Triangle-Squares**, page 44, to complete 12 **triangle-squares**. Repeat with remaining **rectangles** to make a total of 48 **triangle-squares** (12 from each color combination).

Fig. 1

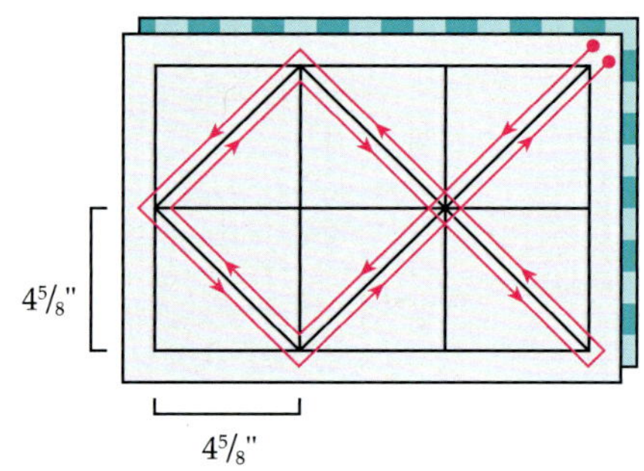

triangle-squares (make 12 of each)

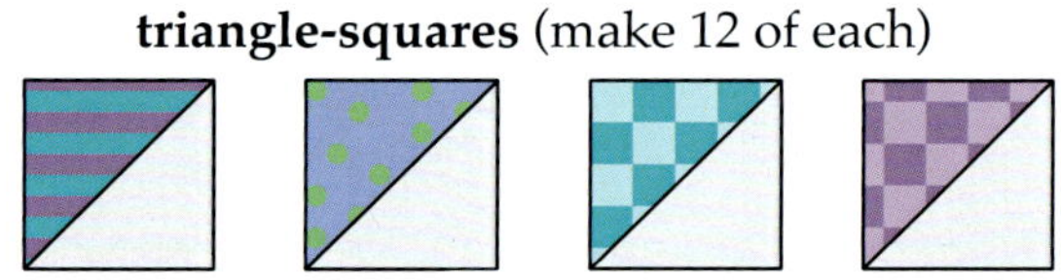

2. Sew 4 **triangle-squares** together to make **Unit 1**. Make 12 **Unit 1's**.

Unit 1 (make 12)

3. Follow **Invisible Appliqué**, page 45, to stitch 1 **circle** to the center of each **Unit 1** to make **Block**. Make 12 **Blocks**.

Block (make 12)

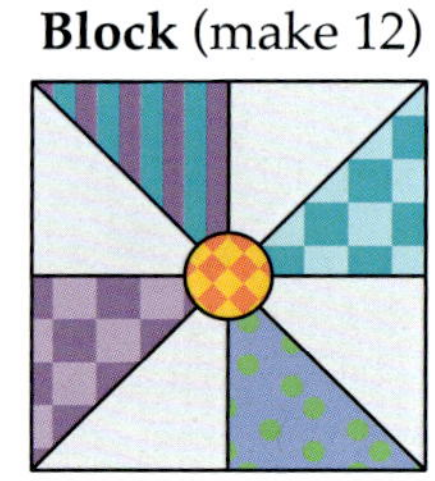

4. Placing appliqués at least 1" from outer edges of **panel**, follow **Invisible Appliqué**, page 45, to stitch **appliqués** to **panel**. Trim **panel** to 8" x 30$^1/_2$" to complete **Appliquéd Panel**. Make 2 **Appliquéd Panels**.

Appliquéd Panel (make 2)

5. Sew 4 **Blocks** together to make **Row**. Make 3 **Rows**.

Row (make 3)

6. Referring to **Quilt Top Diagram**, sew **Rows**, **Appliquéd Panels**, and **sashing strips** together to make center section of quilt top.
7. Sew **side inner borders**, then **side outer borders** to sides of center section.
8. Sew **top/bottom inner borders** to center section.
9. Sew 2 **corner squares**, 2 **sashing pieces**, and 1 **top/bottom outer border** together to make **Border Unit**. Make 2 **Border Units**.

Border Unit (make 2)

10. Sew **Border Units** to top and bottom of center section to complete **Quilt Top**.

COMPLETING THE QUILT

1. Follow **Quilting**, page 47, to mark, layer, and quilt using **Quilting Diagram** as a suggestion.
2. Cut a 22" square of binding fabric. Follow **Binding**, page 49, to bind quilt using 2$^1/_2$"w bias binding with mitered corners.

Quilting Diagram

Quilt Top Diagram

BUMPER PADS

Our bumper pads fit a standard (27" x 52") baby bed.

YARDAGE REQUIREMENTS

Yardage is based on 45"w fabric.

- 3 yds of white print
- $2^1/_4$ yds of blue check
- $^1/_2$ yd of gold check
- $^3/_8$ yd of pink check
- $^1/_8$ yd of purple check
- $^1/_8$ yd of blue dot
- $2^1/_4$ yds of 72"w upholstery batting
- 8 yds of $^1/_4$"w white double-fold bias tape

You will also need:

- transparent monofilament thread for appliqué
- paper-backed fusible web
- $19^1/_2$" x 28" piece of paper (newsprint or craft paper)

CUTTING OUT THE PIECES

*Follow **Rotary Cutting**, page 41, to cut the following pieces, piecing as necessary to obtain indicated lengths.*

1. From white print, cut 4 **side panels** 8" x 53", 2 **foot panels** 8" x 28", and 2 **rectangles** 20" x 29".
2. From blue check, cut 8 **side strips** $2^1/_2$" x 53", 4 **foot strips** $2^1/_2$" x 28", 2 **head strips** $2^1/_2$" x 28", and 2 **rectangles** 14" x 29".

PREPARING THE APPLIQUÉS

*Follow **Preparing Fusible Appliqués**, page 45, and use patterns, page 9, to cut the following **appliqués**.*

1. From purple check, cut 6 **bodies**.
2. From gold check, cut 26 **large stars**, 18 **small stars**, and 6 **moons**.
3. From pink check, cut 32 **small stars**, 6 **tails**, 6 **udders**, 6 **noses**, and 12 **ears** (6 in reverse).
4. From blue dot, cut 6 **heads**.

MAKING THE BUMPER PADS

*Follow **Piecing and Pressing**, page 43, to make bumper pads.*

1. To make head panel pattern, refer to **Fig. 1** to fold paper in half, matching short edges. Mark a point on short edge of paper 10" from bottom. Beginning at top of fold, draw a gentle freehand curve to marked point. Cut through both layers of paper and unfold.

Fig. 1

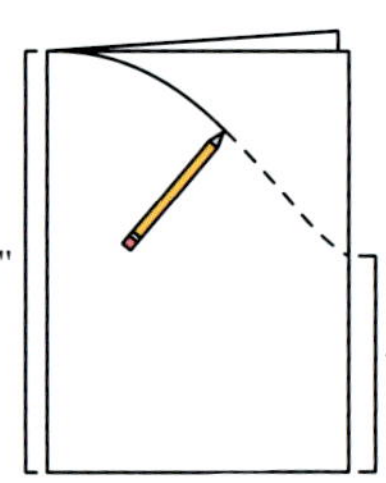

2. Use pattern to cut 2 **head panels** from white print **rectangles**.
3. To make pattern for head panel trim, refer to **Fig. 2** to mark a line $2^1/_2$" from top edge of head panel pattern. Cut along marked line and discard lower portion.

Fig. 2

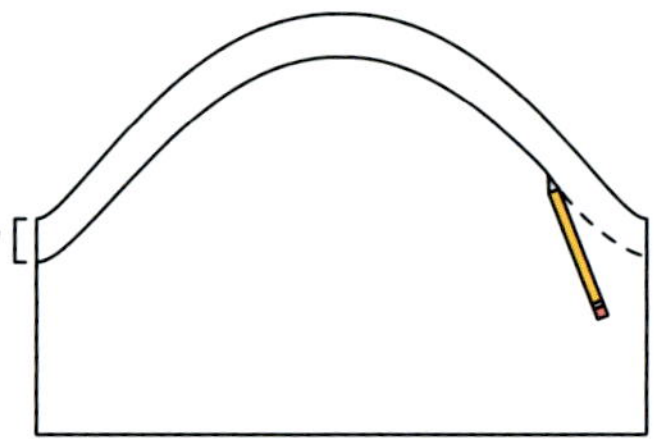

4. Use pattern to cut 2 **head panel trims** from blue check **rectangles**.
5. (***Note:*** Refer to panel diagrams, page 8, for Steps 5 - 8.) Press lower edge of each **head panel trim** $^1/_4$" to wrong side. Matching raw edges, baste wrong side of 1 **head panel trim** to right side of each **head panel** along top edge. Topstitch lower edge of head panel trim to head panel. Sew 1 **head strip** to bottom edge of each **head panel**.
6. Use **head panel** to cut 2 batting pieces.
7. Sew 1 **foot strip** each to top and bottom edges of each **foot panel**. Sew 1 **side strip** each to top and bottom edges of each **side panel**.
8. Follow **Invisible Appliqué**, page 45, to stitch **appliqués** to each **panel**.
9. Cut 4 pieces of batting 12" x 53" and 2 pieces 12" x 28". Baste 1 piece of batting to wrong side of each corresponding **foot**, **side**, and **head panel**.
10. Sewing through all thicknesses, sew 1 **side panel** to each short edge of **foot panel** to make **Bumper Panel**. Make 2 **Bumper Panels**. Trim batting as close as possible to seamlines; trim $^1/_2$" from lower edge of batting.
11. Cut 17 pieces of bias tape 16"l. Fold ends of each piece $^1/_4$" to inside; stitch along long edges. Fold each piece in half to make **ties**.
12. Referring to **Fig. 3**, page 8 (appliqués are not shown), mark each long edge of 1 **Bumper Panel** $26^1/_2$" from ends. Lightly draw a line between marks across width of panel. Baste folded ends of **ties** as shown, adjusting location of ties at marks to fit your bed if necessary.
13. Place **Bumper Panels** right sides together. Using a $^1/_2$" seam allowance, sew pieces together along top and side edges. Trim corners and turn right side out. Turn bottom raw edges $^3/_8$" to inside; topstitch bottom edges together close to edge.
14. Stitch across width of bumper panels (through all thicknesses) along lines marked in Step 12 and along seamlines indicated in **Fig. 3** to complete **Side/Foot Bumper**.

15. Referring to **Fig. 4**, baste 4 **ties** to side edges of 1 **head panel**; baste remaining **tie** to top edge of panel in desired location to fit your bed. Place **head panels** right sides together. Using a 1/2" seam allowance, sew pieces together along top and side edges. Trim 1/2" from lower edge of batting. Trim corners and turn right side out. Turn bottom raw edges of bumpers 3/8" to inside; topstitch bottom edges together close to edge to complete **Head Bumper**.

Fig. 3

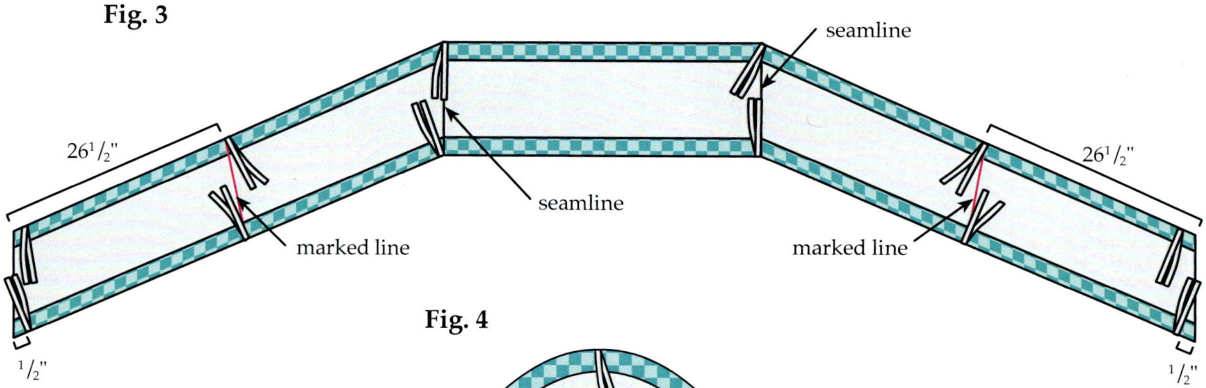

Fig. 4

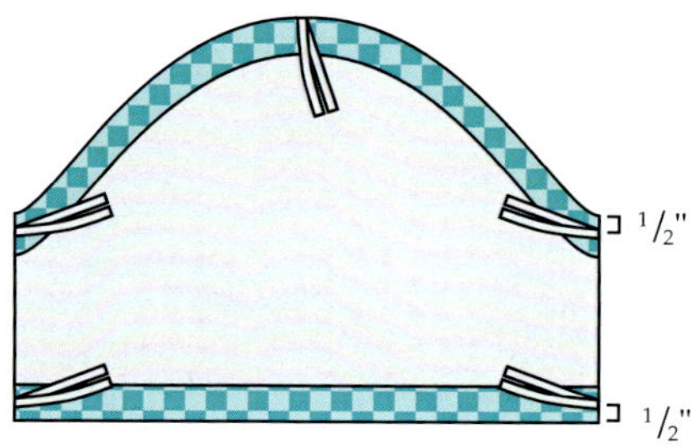

Head Panel (make 2)

Foot Panel (make 2)

Side Panel (make 4)

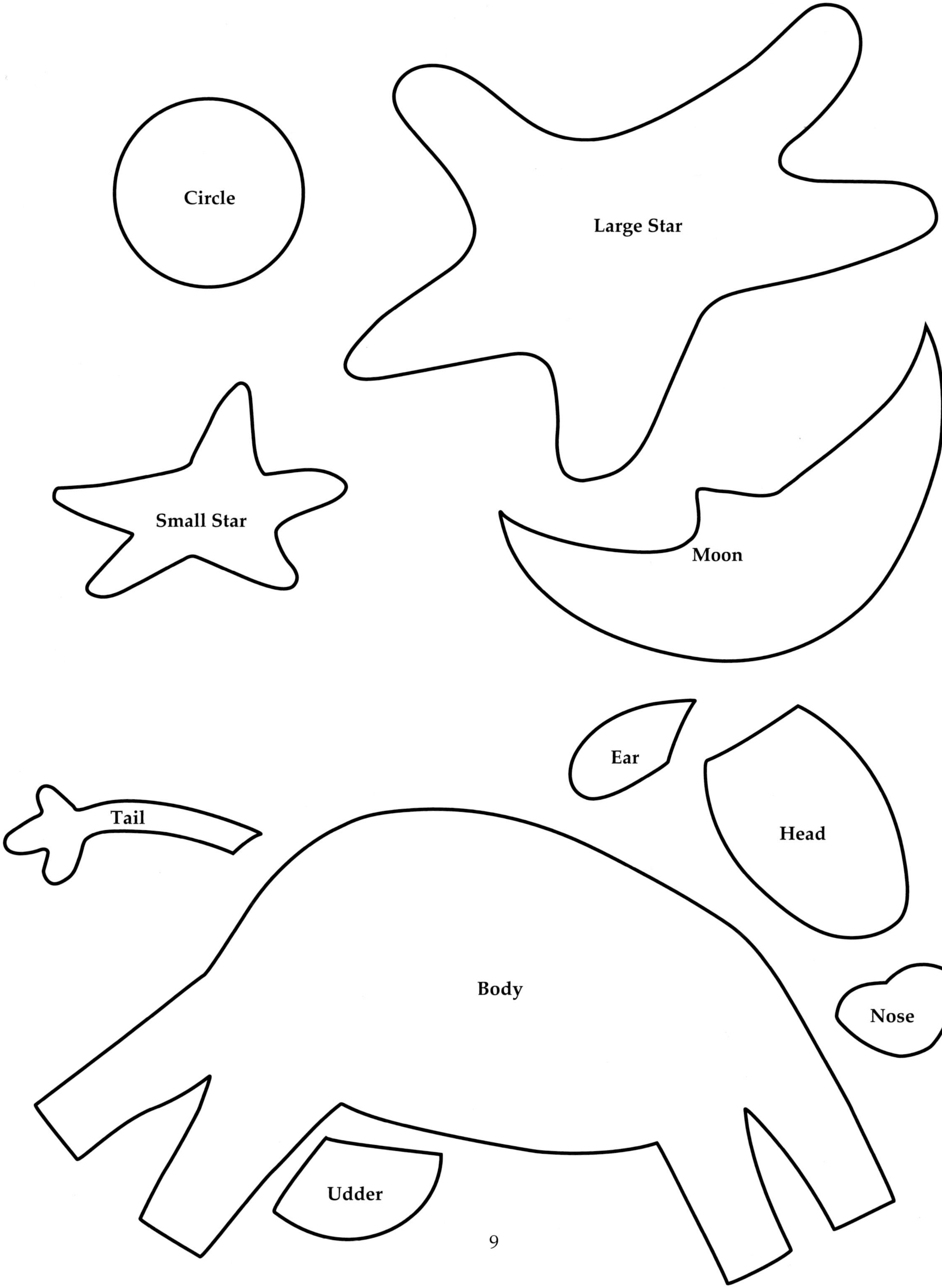
Circle
Large Star
Small Star
Moon
Ear
Tail
Head
Body
Nose
Udder

BOW TIE

CRIB QUILT

BLOCK SIZE: 12" x 12"
QUILT SIZE: 49" x 64"

YARDAGE REQUIREMENTS

Yardage is based on 45"w fabric.

- $1^{1}/_{4}$ yds of light blue solid
- $^{7}/_{8}$ yds of blue stripe
- $^{2}/_{3}$ yd of white solid
- $^{1}/_{2}$ yd of blue print
- $^{1}/_{4}$ yd of dark blue print
- $^{7}/_{8}$ yd of white solid for prairie points
- $2^{7}/_{8}$ yds for backing
- 52" x 67" batting

You will also need:

- tracing paper
- transparent tape
- $^{1}/_{8}$" hole punch
- template plastic

CUTTING OUT THE PIECES

All measurements include a $^{1}/_{4}$" seam allowance.
*Follow **Rotary Cutting**, page 41, to cut fabric.*

1. **From light blue solid:**
   - Cut 3 strips $12^{1}/_{2}$"w. From these strips, cut 31 **sashing strips** $12^{1}/_{2}$" x 3".
2. **From blue stripe:**
   - Cut 4 strips $6^{1}/_{2}$"w. From these strips, cut 24 **large squares** $6^{1}/_{2}$" x $6^{1}/_{2}$".
3. **From white solid:**
   - Cut 4 strips $3^{1}/_{2}$"w. From these strips, cut 48 **square A's** $3^{1}/_{2}$" x $3^{1}/_{2}$".
   - Cut 2 strips 3"w. From these strips, cut 20 **sashing squares** 3" x 3".
4. **From blue print:**
   - Cut 4 strips $3^{1}/_{2}$"w. From these strips, cut 48 **square A's** $3^{1}/_{2}$" x $3^{1}/_{2}$".
5. **From dark blue print:**
   - Cut 2 strips, $2^{5}/_{8}$"w. From these strips, cut 24 **B's** $2^{5}/_{8}$" x $2^{5}/_{8}$".
6. **From white solid for prairie points:**
   - Cut 9 strips 3"w. From these strips, cut 116 **prairie point squares** 3" x 3".

PREPARING BOW TIE PIECES

1. Trace outer edge of Trimming and Marking Template A, page 13, onto tracing paper; cut out. Tape template, right side down, on wrong side of rotary cutting ruler with diagonal edge even with edge of ruler (**Fig. 1**).

Fig. 1

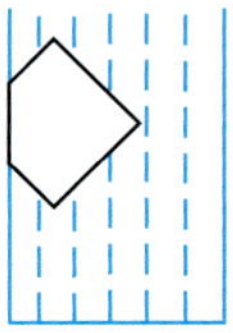

2. To trim corners from **square A's**, place ruler over one square A, matching edges of template to fabric edges (**Fig. 2**). Trim off corner (**Fig. 3**). Trim one corner from all square A's to complete 48 blue **A's** and 48 white **A's**.

Fig. 2

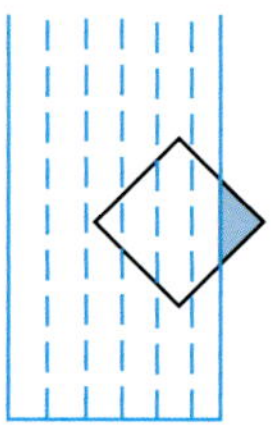

Fig. 3

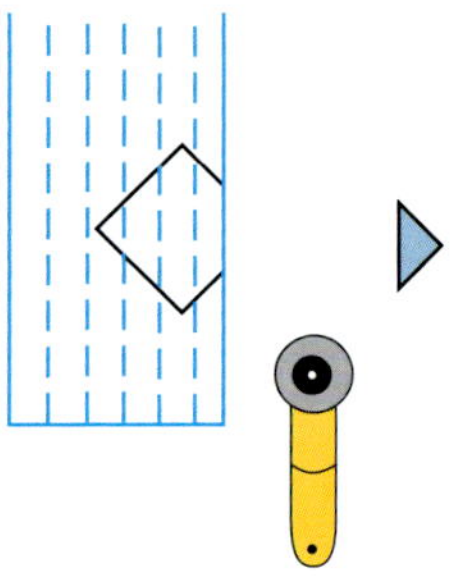

A (make 48)

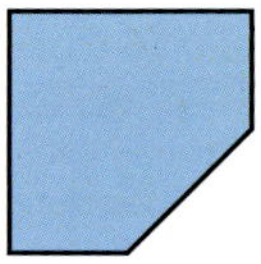

A (make 48)

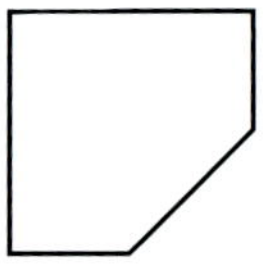

3. Use Trimming and Marking Template A and Marking Template B, page 13, and follow **Template Cutting,** page 43, to cut out templates. Use hole punch to punch holes at dots.
4. To mark starting and stopping points for stitching, place marking template on wrong side of 1 A and mark dots through holes (**Fig. 4**). Repeat for all A's and B's.

Fig. 4

ASSEMBLING THE QUILT TOP

*Follow **Piecing and Pressing**, page 43, to make quilt top.*

1. Making sure to stitch between the dots only, sew 2 blue **A's** and 1 **B** together to make **Unit 1**. Make 24 **Unit 1's**.

Unit 1 (make 24)

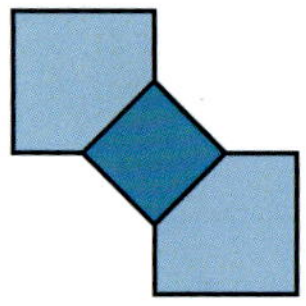

2. To make Unit 2, pin 1 white **A** to 1 **Unit 1**, carefully matching dots. Stitch seam from the outer edge to the dot at the inside corner (**Fig. 5**).

Fig. 5

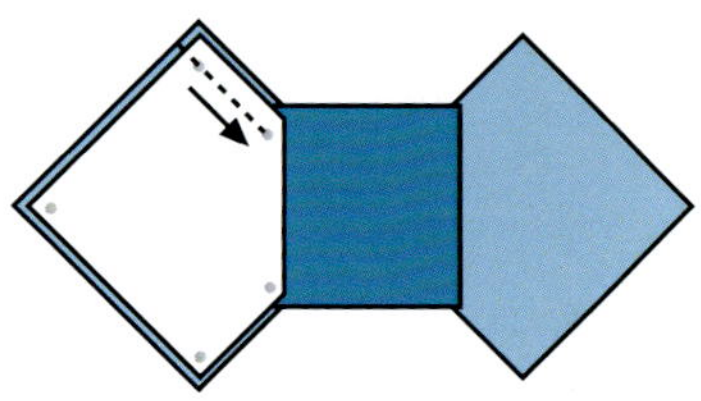

3. Pivot the added piece in order to sew the second seam. Pin and sew as before, beginning with the needle in the hole of the last stitch taken and ending at the second dot **(Fig. 6)**.

Fig. 6

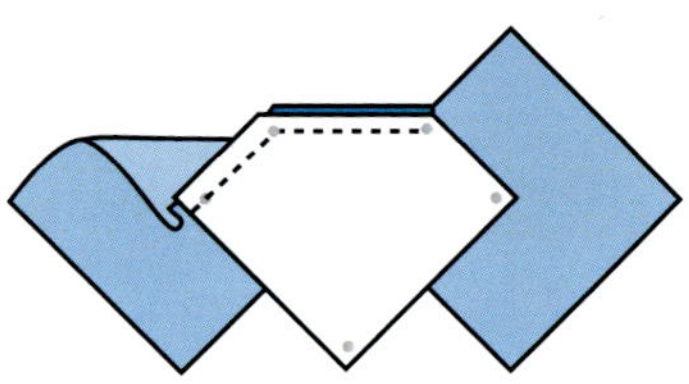

4. Pivot the added piece again and stitch remainder of seam from dot to outer edge, beginning with the needle in the hole of the last stitch taken (**Fig. 7**).

Fig. 7

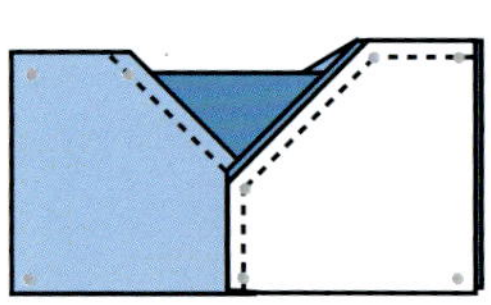

5. Repeat Steps 2-4 to make a total of 24 **Unit 2's.**

Unit 2 (make 24)

6. Sew 2 **Unit 2's** and 2 **large squares** together to make **Block**. Make 12 **Blocks.**

Block (make 12)

7. Sew 4 **sashing strips** and 3 **Blocks** together to make **Block Row**. Make 4 **Block Rows.**

Block Row (make 4)

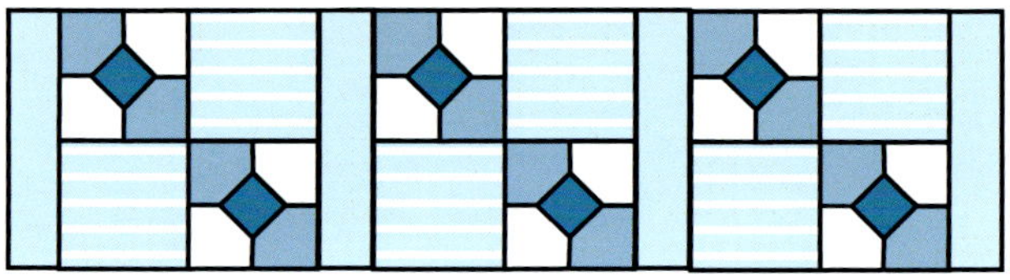

8. Sew 4 **sashing squares** and 3 **sashing strips** together to make **Sashing Row**. Make 5 **Sashing Rows**.

Sashing Row (make 5)

9. Sew **Sashing Rows** and **Block Rows** together to complete **Quilt Top**.

COMPLETING THE QUILT

1. For each prairie point, press **prairie point square** in half with wrong sides together (**Fig. 8**). Press in half again (**Fig. 9**).

Fig. 8

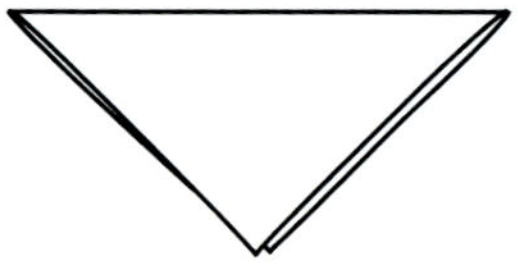

Fig. 9

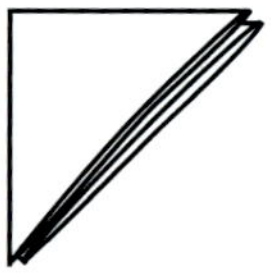

2. Beginning at corner, pin 25 prairie points to each short edge (**Fig. 10**) and 33 prairie points to each long edge. Stitch in place. Press prairie points out.

Fig. 10

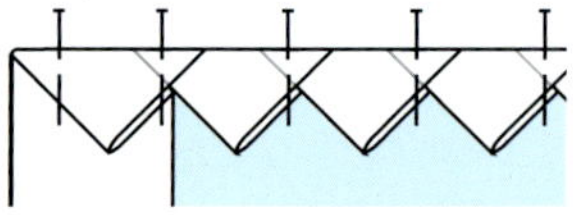

3. Follow **Quilting**, page 47, to mark, layer, and quilt, using **Quilting Diagram** as a suggestion.
4. Trim batting even with seamline of prairie points. Trim backing $^{1}/_{4}$" larger than batting. Press edges of backing $^{1}/_{4}$" to wrong side. Blindstitch backing to quilt.

Quilting Diagram

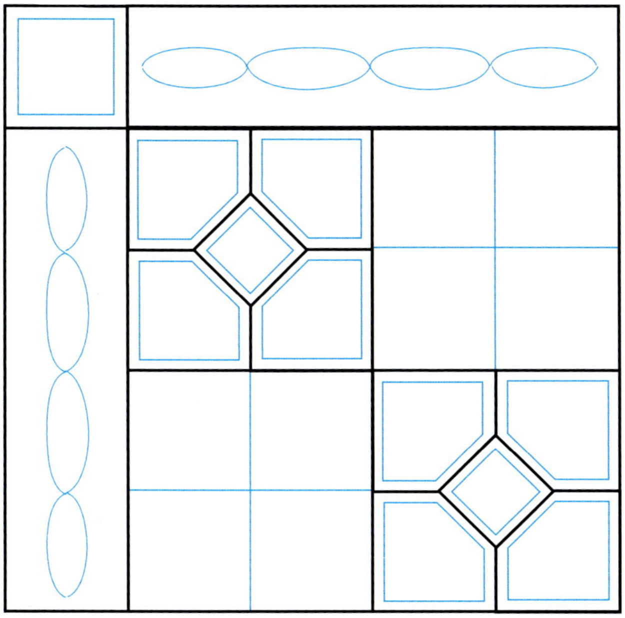

Quilt Top Diagram

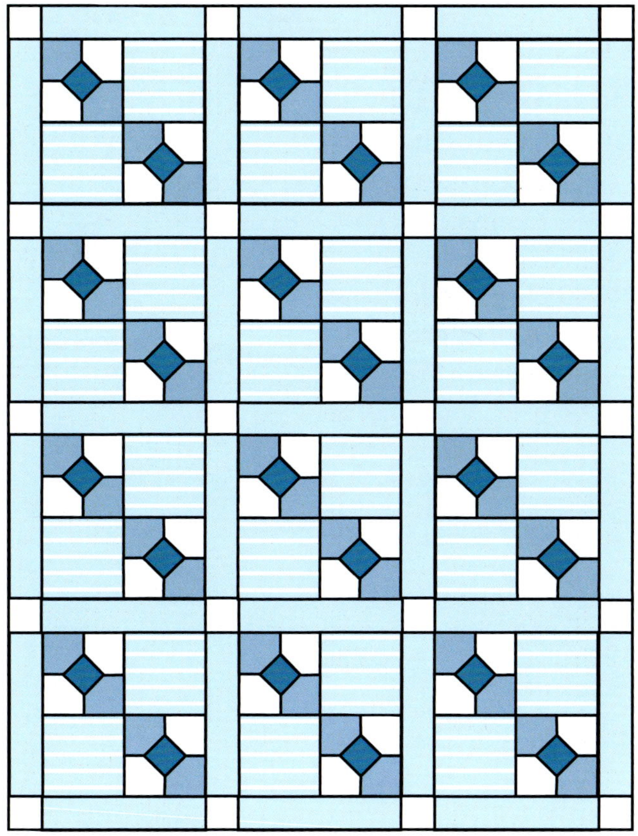

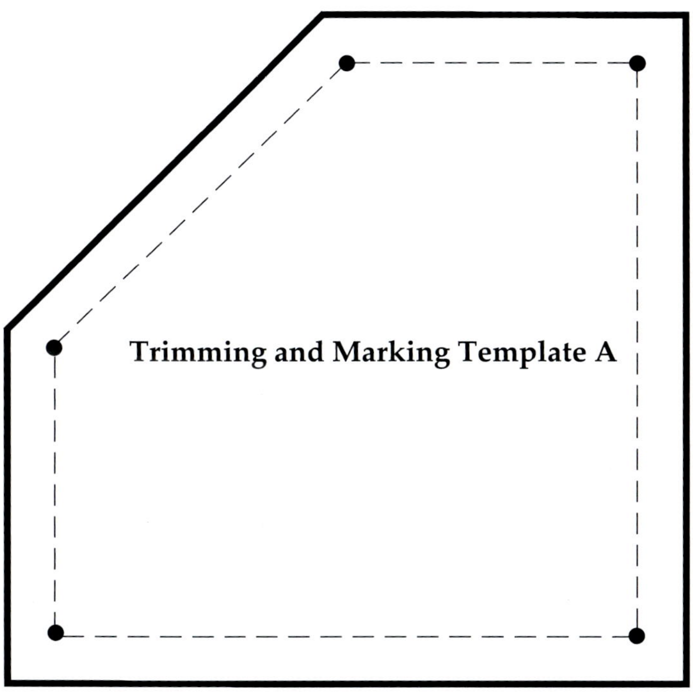

SPRINGTIME

CRIB QUILT

QUILT SIZE: 41" x 51"

YARDAGE REQUIREMENTS

Yardage is based on 45"w fabric.

- $1^3/_4$ yds of white solid
- $^3/_8$ yd of pale yellow solid
- $^1/_2$ yd of green check
- $^1/_4$ yd of light pink print
- $^1/_4$ yd of medium pink print
- $^1/_4$ yd of dark pink print
- $2^3/_4$ yds for backing
- $^3/_4$ yd for binding
- 48" x 60" batting

You will also need:

- paper-backed fusible web
- transparent monofilament thread for appliqué
- plastic template material
- craft knife
- green fabric paint
- stencil brush

CUTTING OUT THE PIECES

*All measurements include a $^1/_4$" seam allowance. Follow **Rotary Cutting**, page 41, to cut fabric.*

1. **From white solid:**
   - Cut 2 **strips** $2^1/_2$"w.
   - Cut 2 **side outer borders** $6^1/_2$" x $36^1/_2$".
   - Cut 2 **top/bottom outer borders** $6^1/_2$" x $26^1/_2$".
   - Cut 2 **panels** $9^1/_2$" x $26^1/_2$".
2. **From pale yellow solid:**
   - Cut 4 **strips** $2^1/_2$"w.
3. **From green check:**
   - Cut 1 strip $1^1/_4$"w. From this strip, cut 4 **border pieces** $1^1/_4$" x $6^1/_2$".
   - Cut 2 **top/bottom inner borders** $1^1/_4$" x 40".
   - Cut 2 **side inner borders** $1^1/_4$" x $36^1/_2$".
4. **From 3 pink prints:**
   - Cut 2 **strips** $2^1/_2$"w from **each** fabric.

ASSEMBLING THE QUILT TOP

*Follow **Piecing and Pressing**, page 43, to make quilt top.*

1. (*Note:* Measurements for stencil placement on **Quilt Top Diagram** do not include seam allowances.) Referring to **Quilt Top Diagram**, page 16, use **Stem Stencil** pattern, page 19, and follow **Stenciling**, page 52, to stencil stems on **outer borders**. Stencil stems on **panels**, using only 2 segments of stem stencil for each design area.
2. Use patterns and follow **Preparing Fusible Appliqués**, page 45, to cut 32 **leaves** and 4 **flower bases** from green check, 4 **flower petals** from light pink print, 10 **hearts** from medium pink print, and 8 **flower petals** from dark pink print. Follow **Invisible Appliqué**, page 45, to stitch appliqués to **panels** and **outer borders**.
3. Sew pale yellow and dark pink print **strips** together to make **Strip Set A**. Make 2 **Strip Set A's**. Cut across **Strip Set A's** at $2^1/_2$" intervals to make 29 **Unit 1's**. Repeat with light pink print, medium pink print, and white **strips** to make 2 **Strip Set B's** and 22 **Unit 2's**.

Strip Set A (make 2)

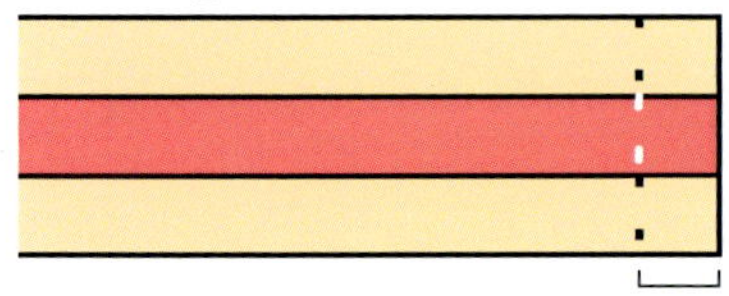

Unit 1 (make 29)

Strip Set B (make 2)

Unit 2 (make 22)

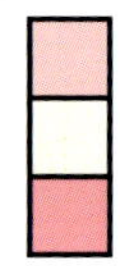

4. Sew 7 **Unit 1's** and 6 **Unit 2's** together to make **Row**. Make 3 **Rows**.

Row (make 3)

5. Sew 2 **Unit 1's** and 1 **Unit 2** together to make **Border Square**. Make 4 **Border Squares**.

Border Square (make 4)

6. Referring to **Quilt Top Diagram**, page 16, sew **Rows** and **panels** together to make center section of quilt top.
7. Sew **side inner borders**, then **side outer borders** to center section.
8. Sew 2 **Border Squares**, 2 **border pieces**, and 1 **top/bottom outer border** together to make **Border Unit**. Make 2 **Border Units**.
9. Sew **top/bottom inner borders**, then **Border Units** to center section to complete **Quilt Top**.

COMPLETING THE QUILT

1. Follow **Quilting**, page 47, to mark, layer, and quilt, using **Quilting Diagram** as a suggestion.
2. Follow **Binding**, page 49, to bind quilt using 4"w straight-grain binding with overlapped corners.

Quilting Diagram

Quilt Top Diagram

BUMPER PADS

Our bumper pads fit a standard (27" x 52") baby bed.

YARDAGE REQUIREMENTS

Yardage is based on 45"w fabric.

- 3 yds of white solid
- $2^1/_4$ yds of green check
- $^1/_4$ yd of light pink print
- $^1/_4$ yd of medium pink print
- $^1/_4$ yd of dark pink print
- $2^1/_4$ yds of 72"w upholstery batting
- 8 yds of $^1/_4$"w white double-fold bias tape

You will also need:

- transparent monofilament thread for appliqué
- paper-backed fusible web
- $19^1/_2$" x 28" piece of paper (newsprint or craft paper)
- plastic template material
- craft knife
- green fabric paint
- stencil brush

CUTTING OUT THE PIECES

Follow ***Rotary Cutting****, page 41, to cut the following pieces, piecing as necessary to obtain indicated lengths.*

1. From white solid, cut 4 **side panels** 8" x 53", 2 **foot panels** 8" x 28", and 2 **rectangles** 20" x 29".
2. From green check, cut 8 **side strips** $2^1/_2$" x 53", 4 **foot strips** $2^1/_2$" x 28", 2 **head strips** $2^1/_2$" x 28", and 2 **rectangles** 14" x 29".

PREPARING THE APPLIQUÉS

Follow ***Preparing Fusible Appliqués****, page 45, and use patterns, page 19, to cut the following* ***appliqués****.*

1. From light pink print, cut 24 **flower petals**.
2. From medium pink print, cut 20 **hearts**.
3. From dark pink print, cut 48 **flower petals**.
4. From green check, cut 24 **flower bases** and 48 **leaves**.

MAKING THE BUMPER PADS

Follow ***Piecing and Pressing****, page 43, to make bumper pads.*

1. To make head panel pattern, refer to **Fig. 1** to fold paper in half, matching short edges. Mark a point on short edge of paper 10" from bottom. Beginning at top of fold, draw a gentle freehand curve to marked point. Cut through both layers of paper and unfold.

Fig. 1

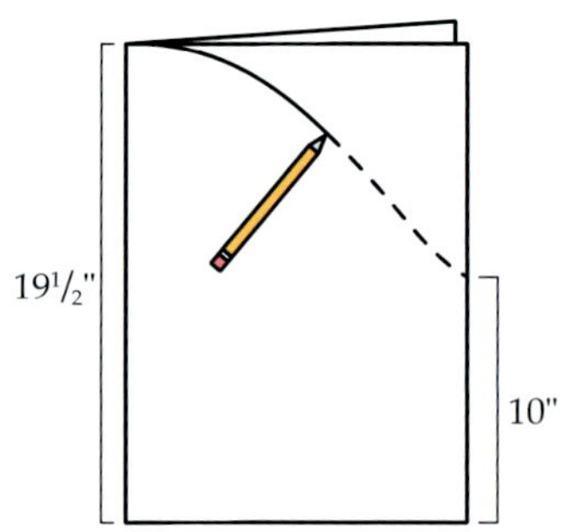

2. Use pattern to cut 2 **head panels** from white solid **rectangles**.
3. (*Note*: Measurements for stencil placement on **Head Panel**, **Foot Panel**, and **Side Panel** diagrams, this page and page 19, do not include seam allowances.) Referring to diagrams, use **Stem Stencil** pattern and follow **Stenciling**, page 52, to stencil stems.
4. To make pattern for head panel trim, refer to **Fig. 2** to mark a line $2^1/_2$" from top edge of head panel pattern. Cut along marked line and discard lower portion.

Fig. 2

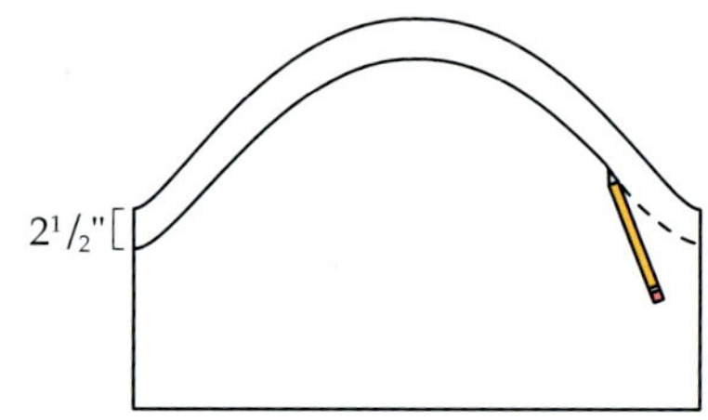

5. Use pattern to cut 2 **head panel trims** from green check **rectangles**.
6. (*Note:* Refer to panel diagrams for Steps 6 - 9.) Press lower edge of each **head panel trim** $^1/_4$" to wrong side. Matching raw edges, baste wrong side of 1 **head panel trim** to right side of each **head panel** along top edge. Topstitch lower edge of head panel trim to head panel. Sew 1 **head strip** to bottom edge of each **head panel**.
7. Use head panel to cut 2 batting pieces.
8. Sew 1 **foot strip** each to top and bottom edges of each **foot panel**. Sew 1 **side strip** to top and bottom edges of each **side panel**.
9. Follow **Invisible Appliqué**, page 45, to stitch **appliqués** to each **panel**.
10. Follow Steps 9-14 of **Nursery Rhyme Bumper Pads**, page 6, to complete pads.

Head Panel (make 2)

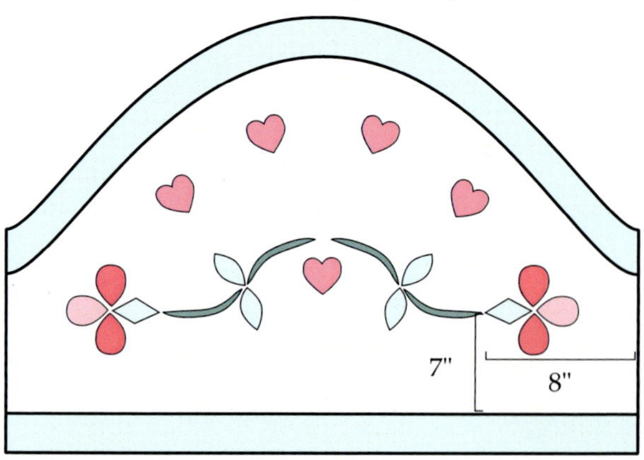

Side Panel (make 4)

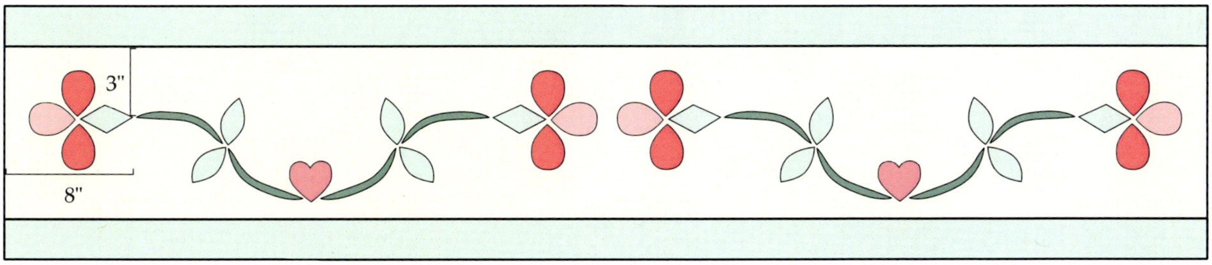

Foot Panel (make 2)

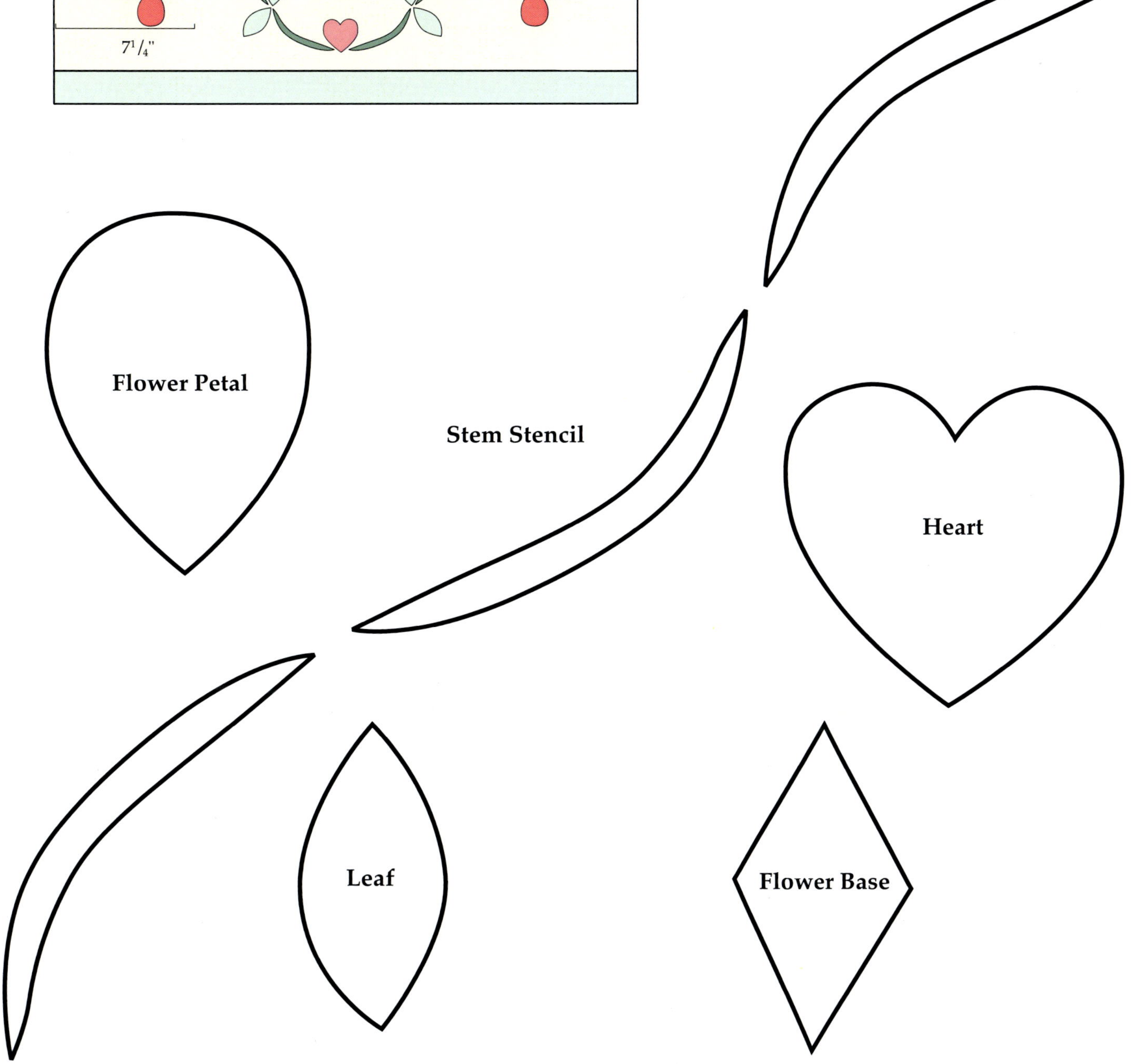

SWEET DREAMS

CRIB QUILT

BLOCK SIZE: 7" x 7"
QUILT SIZE: 35" x 35"

YARDAGE REQUIREMENTS

Yardage is based on 45"w fabric.

- $^7/_8$ yd of white check
- $^1/_2$ yd of blue dot
- $^1/_4$ yd of yellow check
- $^1/_4$ yd **each** of 5 pastel prints
- $^1/_4$ yd of light brown print
- 1 yd of $^1/_2$"w flat lace trim
- $1^1/_4$ yds for backing
- $^5/_8$ yd for binding
- 45" x 60" batting

You will also need:

- paper-backed fusible web
- tracing paper
- iron-on transfer pen
- black permanent fabric marker
- cream fabric paint
- small paintbrush
- transparent monofilament thread for appliqué

CUTTING OUT THE PIECES

All measurements include a $^1/_4$" seam allowance. Follow ***Rotary Cutting****, page 41, to cut fabric.*

1. **From white check:**
   - Cut 2 strips $3^1/_2$"w. From these strips, cut 9 **rectangles** $3^1/_2$" x $7^1/_2$".
   - Cut 4 strips $4^1/_2$"w. From these strips, cut 2 **top/bottom borders** $4^1/_2$" x $25^1/_2$" and 2 **side borders** $4^1/_2$" x $33^1/_2$".
2. **From blue dot:**
   - Cut 4 strips $1^1/_2$"w. From these strips, cut 16 **sashing pieces** $1^1/_2$" x $7^1/_2$".
   - Cut 1 **large rectangle** $7^1/_2$" x 18".
3. **From yellow check:**
   - Cut 1 strip $1^1/_2$"w. Cut strip in half to make 2 **sashing strips**.
4. **From pastel prints and remaining yellow check:**
   - Cut a total of 4 **strips** $1^1/_2$"w for Heart Blocks.
   - Cut a total of 5 **blankets** $4^1/_2$" x $7^1/_2$".
5. **From flat lace trim:**
   - Cut 4 **lace pieces** $7^1/_2$"l.

PREPARING THE APPLIQUÉS

1. **To make pillows:**
   - Follow **Preparing Fusible Appliqués**, page 45, to cut a total of 5 **pillows** $1^3/_4$" x $4^1/_4$" from pastel prints.
2. **To make hearts:**
   - Use **Heart Pattern**, page 27, and follow **Preparing Fusible Appliqués**, page 45, to make 4 **hearts** from 1 pastel print.
3. **To make bears:**
   - Follow **Preparing Fusible Appliqués**, page 45, to cut 5 rectangles 6" x 7" from light brown print.
   - Use transfer pen to trace **Bear Pattern**, page 27, onto tracing paper. Follow transfer pen manufacturer's instructions to transfer pattern to right side of each rectangle.
   - Referring to photo, use black fabric marker to darken inner detail lines on bears. Use paintbrush to dab cream paint on nose, paws, and inner ears.
   - Cut out **bears** along outer lines.

ASSEMBLING THE QUILT TOP

Follow ***Piecing and Pressing****, page 43, to make quilt top.*

1. Sew 1 **rectangle** and 1 **blanket** together to make **Unit 1**. Make 5 **Unit 1's**.

Unit 1 (make 5)

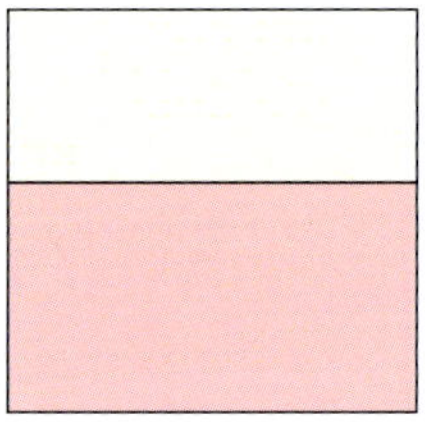

2. Sew **strips** together to make 1 **Strip Set A**. Cut across **Strip Set A** at $7^1/_2$" intervals to make 4 **Unit 2's**.

Strip Set A (make 1)

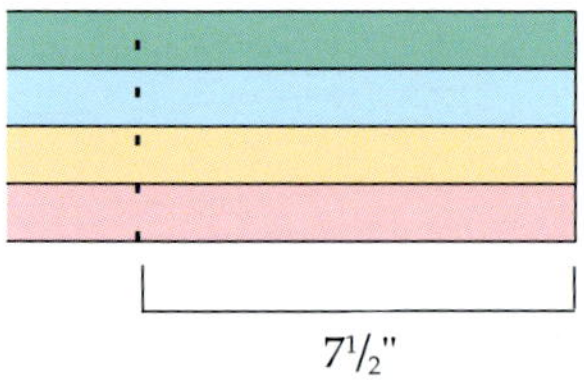

Unit 2 (make 4)

3. Follow **Invisible Appliqué**, page 45, to stitch **pillow** and **bear** to **Unit 1** to make **Bear Block**. Make 5 **Bear Blocks**.

Bear Block (make 5)

4. Follow **Invisible Appliqué**, page 45, to stitch **hearts** to remaining **rectangles**, matching bottom edges of **hearts** and **rectangles**.

5. Sew 1 **Unit 2** and 1 **rectangle** together. Topstitch 1 **lace piece** along top of green strip to make **Heart Block**. Make 4 **Heart Blocks**.

Heart Block (make 4)

6. Assemble **large rectangle** and **sashing strips** to make 1 **Strip Set B** (ends will be uneven). Cut across **Strip Set B** at $1^{1}/_{2}$" intervals to make 8 **Unit 4's**.

Strip Set B (make 1)

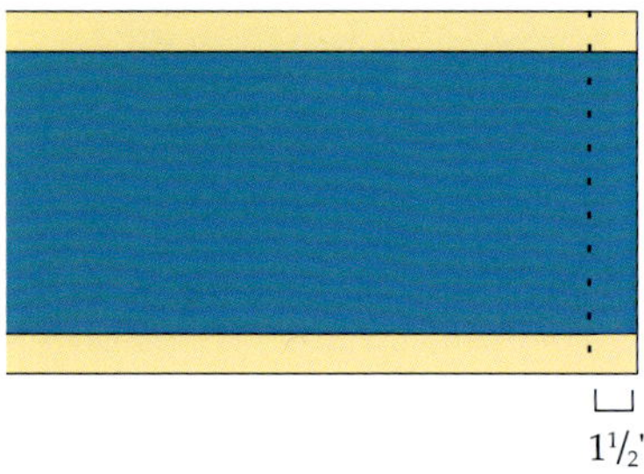

Unit 4 (make 8)

7. Assemble 2 **Unit 4's** and 1 **sashing piece** to make **Sashing Unit**. Make 4 **Sashing Units**.

Sashing Unit (make 4)

8. Assemble 4 **sashing pieces**, 2 **Bear Blocks**, and 1 **Heart Block** to make **Row A**. Make 2 **Row A's**.

Row A (make 2)

9. Assemble 4 **sashing pieces**, 2 **Heart Blocks**, and 1 **Bear Block** to make 1 **Row B**.

Row B (make 1)

10. Referring to **Quilt Top Diagram**, sew **Sashing Units**, **Row A's**, and **Row B** together to complete center section of quilt top.
11. Sew **top**, **bottom**, then **side borders** to center section to complete **Quilt Top**.

COMPLETING THE QUILT

1. Follow **Quilting**, page 47, to mark, layer, and quilt, using **Quilting Diagram** as a suggestion.
2. Follow **Binding**, page 49, to bind quilt using $4^{1}/_{2}$"w straight-grain binding with overlapped corners. When preparing quilt for binding, trim backing and batting a scant $^{3}/_{4}$" larger than quilt top.

Quilting Diagram

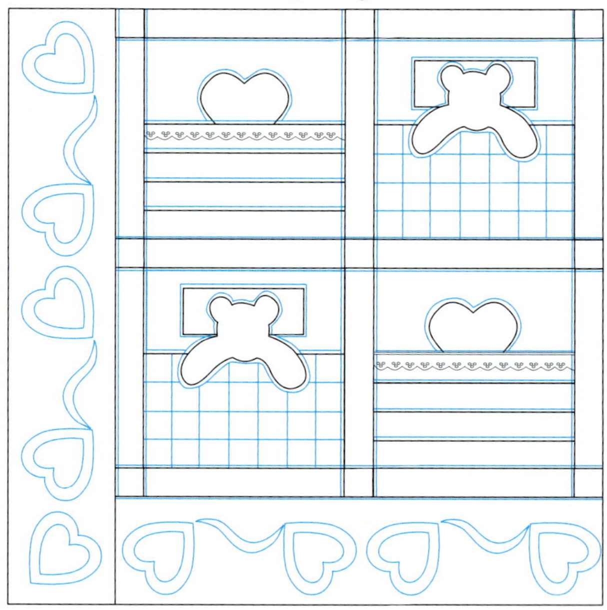

Quilt Top Diagram

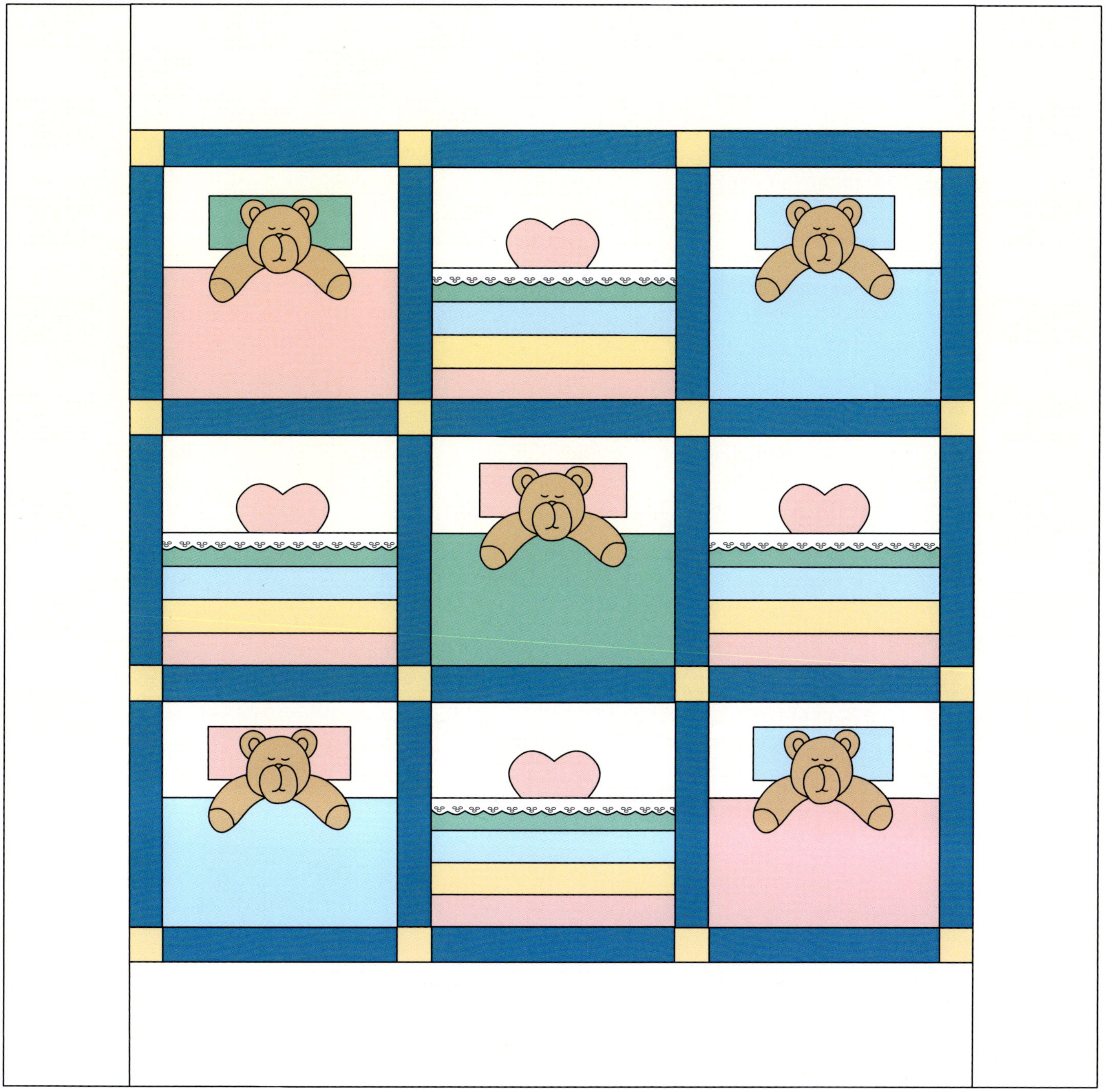

WALL HANGING

WALL HANGING SIZE: 17" x 25"

YARDAGE REQUIREMENTS

Yardage is based on 45"w fabric.

- 1/4 yd of white check
- 1/4 yd of dark brown print
- 1/8 yd **each** of 6 pastel prints
- 1/8 yd of white print
- scrap of light brown print
- 1/4 yd of 1/2"w flat lace trim
- 1/2 yd for backing and hanging sleeve
- 1/4 yd for binding
- 20" x 28" batting

You will also need:

- paper-backed fusible web
- tracing paper
- iron-on transfer pen
- black and brown permanent fabric markers
- cream fabric paint
- 2 brown 5/8" buttons
- small paintbrush
- transparent monofilament thread for appliqué

CUTTING OUT THE PIECES

*All measurements include a 1/4" seam allowance. Follow **Rotary Cutting**, page 41, to cut fabric unless otherwise indicated.*

1. **From white check:**
   - Cut 2 strips 2 1/2"w. From these strips, cut 2 **top/bottom inner borders** 2 1/2" x 8 1/2" and 2 **side inner borders** 2 1/2" x 20 1/2".
   - Follow **Preparing Fusible Appliqués**, page 45, to cut 1 **pillow** 1 3/4" x 4 1/4".
2. **From dark brown print:**
   - Cut 1 **headboard** 3 1/2" x 7 1/2".
   - Cut 1 **footboard** 1 1/2" x 7 1/2".
   - Cut 1 strip 1"w. From this strip, cut 2 **bedposts** 1" x 16 1/2".
3. **From pastel prints:**
   - Cut a total of 6 **blanket pieces** 1 1/2" x 7 1/2".
   - Cut a total of 4 strips 2 1/2" x 24". Cut across strips at 2 1/2" intervals to make 36 **squares** for pieced borders.
4. **From white print:**
   - Cut 1 **lower piece** 3 1/4" x 7 1/2".
   - Cut 1 **middle piece** 1 1/2" x 7 1/2".
   - Cut 1 **upper piece** 2 3/4" x 7 1/2".
5. **From light brown print:**
   - Follow **Preparing Fusible Appliqués**, page 45, to cut 1 rectangle 6" x 7".
   - Use transfer pen to trace **Bear Pattern**, page 27, onto tracing paper. Follow transfer pen manufacturer's instructions to transfer pattern to right side of rectangle.
   - Referring to photo, use black fabric marker to darken inner detail lines on bear. Use paintbrush to dab cream paint on nose, paws, and inner ears.
   - Cut out bear along outer lines.

ASSEMBLING THE WALL HANGING TOP

*Follow **Piecing and Pressing**, page 43, to make wall hanging top.*

1. Sew together **upper piece**, **headboard**, **middle piece**, **blanket pieces**, **footboard**, and **lower piece** to make **Center Panel**.

Center Panel

2. Sew lace across top of blue **blanket piece** and trim off excess. Sew **bedposts** to sides of **Center Panel**. Follow **Invisible Appliqué**, page 45, to stitch **pillow** and **bear** in place to make **Bed Unit**.

Bed Unit

3. (*Note:* Refer to **Wall Hanging Top Diagram**, page 26, for Steps 3 - 5.) Sew **top**, **bottom**, then **side inner borders** to **Bed Unit** to make center section of wall hanging top.
4. Sew 6 squares together for each **top/bottom pieced border** and 12 **squares** together for each **side pieced border**.
5. Sew **top**, **bottom**, then **side pieced borders** to center section to complete **Wall Hanging Top**.

beary sweet dreams
beary sweet dreams

COMPLETING THE WALL HANGING

1. Referring to photo, use **Sweet Dreams Pattern**, page 27, and brown fabric marker to trace words onto **inner borders**.
2. Follow **Quilting**, page 47, to mark, layer, and quilt, using **Quilting Diagram** as a suggestion.
3. Sew buttons to tops of **bedposts**.
4. For hanging sleeve, cut a piece of fabric 7" x 24". Press short edges of fabric piece $^1/_4$" to wrong side; press edges to wrong side $^1/_4$" again and machine stitch in place.
5. Matching wrong sides, fold piece in half lengthwise to form a tube. Matching raw edges, baste hanging sleeve to center top edge on back of wall hanging.
6. Follow **Binding**, page 49, to bind wall hanging using 2"w straight-grain binding with overlapped corners. When preparing wall hanging for binding, trim backing and batting even with wall hanging top.
7. Blindstitch bottom of hanging sleeve in place, taking care not to stitch through to front of wall hanging.
8. Insert a dowel or slat into hanging sleeve.

Quilting Diagram

Wall Hanging Top Diagram

beary
sweet
dreams...

Heart Pattern

Bear Pattern

DRESDEN PLATE

CRIB QUILT

BLOCK SIZE: 12" x 12"
QUILT SIZE: 49" x 64"

YARDAGE REQUIREMENTS

Yardage is based on 45"w fabric.

$2^{1}/_{4}$ yds of pink solid
$1^{3}/_{4}$ yds of white solid
$^{7}/_{8}$ yd of pink print
$^{3}/_{4}$ yd of organdy or other very lightweight cotton fabric
$^{7}/_{8}$ yd of white solid for prairie points
$2^{7}/_{8}$ yds for backing
52" x 67" batting

You will also need:

transparent monofilament thread for appliqué
pinking shears (optional)

CUTTING OUT THE PIECES

All measurements include a $^{1}/_{4}$" seam allowance. Follow **Rotary Cutting**, *page 41, and* **Template Cutting**, *page 43, to cut fabric.*

1. **From pink solid:**
   - Cut 3 strips $12^{1}/_{2}$"w. From these strips, cut 31 **sashing strips** $12^{1}/_{2}$" x 3".
   - Cut 96 **A's** using Template A, page 31.
   - Cut 12 **B's** using Template B, page 31.
2. **From white solid:**
   - Cut 4 strips $12^{1}/_{2}$"w. From these strips, cut 12 **background squares** $12^{1}/_{2}$" x $12^{1}/_{2}$".
   - Cut 2 strips 3"w. From these strips, cut 20 **sashing squares** 3" x 3".
3. **From pink print:**
   - Cut 96 **A's** using Template A, page 31.
4. **From organdy:**
   - Cut 6 strips 3"w. From these strips, cut 192 **lining rectangles** 3" x $1^{1}/_{4}$".
   - Cut 12 **B's** using Template B, page 31.
5. **From white solid for prairie points:**
   - Cut 9 strips 3"w. From these strips, cut 116 **prairie point squares** 3" x 3".

ASSEMBLING THE QUILT TOP

Follow **Piecing and Pressing**, *page 43, to make quilt top.*

1. Referring to **Fig. 1**, place 1 **lining rectangle** and 1 **A** right sides together. Stitch from dot to dot $^{1}/_{4}$" from curved edge of A, backstitching at beginning and end of seam. Repeat with remaining **A's**.

Fig. 1

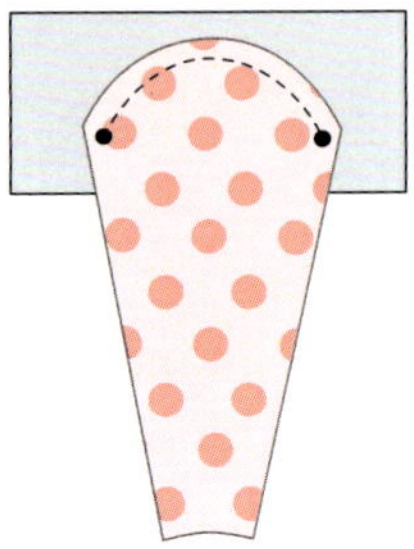

2. Referring to **Fig. 2**, trim excess lining fabric even with side edges of **A;** use pinking shears to trim seam allowance along curve to $^{1}/_{8}$" (trim to $^{1}/_{8}$" and clip curve if not using pinking shears). Turn right side out; press. Repeat with remaining **A's**.

Fig. 2 **A** (make 96) **A** (make 96)

3. Alternating colors, sew 16 **A's** together to make **Unit 1**. Make 12 **Unit 1's**.

Unit 1 (make 12)

4. Place 1 pink **B** and 1 organdy **B** right sides together; stitch $^{1}/_{4}$" from edge. Use pinking shears to trim seam allowance to $^{1}/_{8}$". To make opening for turning, cut a slit in organdy only (**Fig. 3**). Turn right side out and press. Repeat with remaining **B's**.

Fig. 3

B (Make 12)

5. Center 1 **B** over hole in center of 1 **Unit 1**. Follow **Mock Hand Appliqué**, page 46, to stitch **B** to **Unit 1** to make **Unit 2**. Make 12 **Unit 2's**.

Unit 2 (make 12)

6. Fold **background square** in half twice and press folds; unfold. Using pressed lines as placement guidelines, center **Unit 2** on **background square**. Follow **Mock Hand Appliqué**, page 46, to stitch **Unit 2** to **background square** to complete **Block**. Make 12 **Blocks**.

Block (make 12)

7. Sew 4 **sashing strips** and 3 **Blocks** together to make **Block Row**. Make 4 **Block Rows.**

Block Row (make 4)

8. Sew 4 **sashing squares** and 3 **sashing strips** together to make **Sashing Row**. Make 5 **Sashing Rows**.

Sashing Row (make 5)

9. Sew **Sashing Rows** and **Block Rows** together to complete **Quilt Top**.

COMPLETING THE QUILT

1. For each prairie point, press **prairie point square** in half with wrong sides together (**Fig. 4**). Press in half again (**Fig. 5**).

Fig. 4

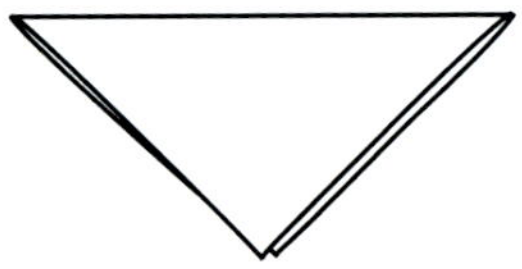

Fig. 5

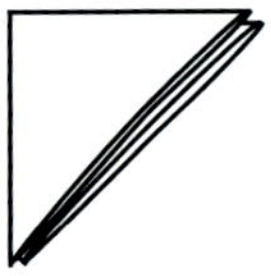

2. Beginning at corner, pin 25 prairie points to each short edge (**Fig. 6**) and 33 prairie points to each long edge. Stitch in place. Press prairie points out.

Fig. 6

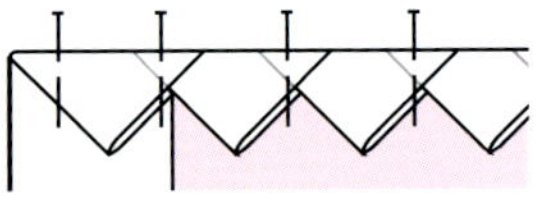

3. Follow **Quilting**, page 47, to mark, layer, and quilt, using **Quilting Diagram**, page 31, as a suggestion.
4. Trim batting even with seamline of prairie points. Trim backing $^{1}/_{4}$" larger than batting. Press edges of backing $^{1}/_{4}$" to wrong side. Blindstitch backing to quilt.

Quilting Diagram

Quilt Top Diagram

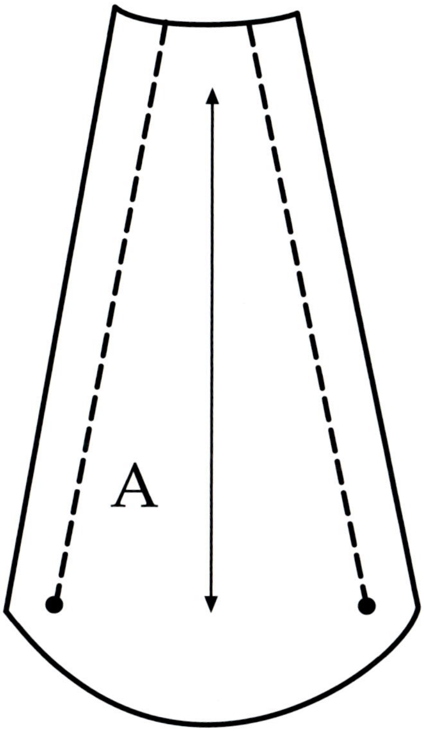

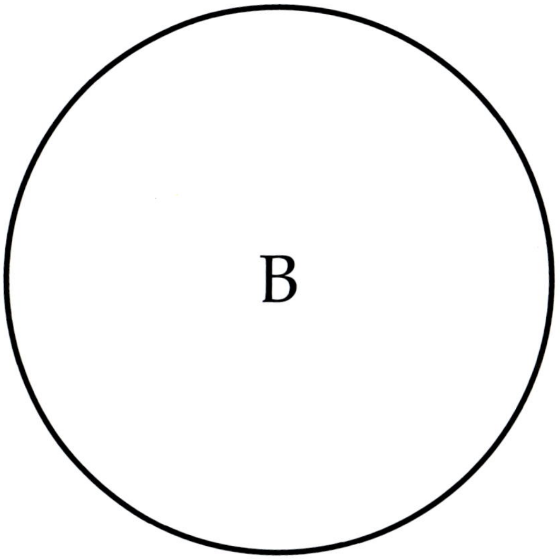

CHOO-CHOO

CRIB QUILT

BLOCK SIZE: $6^{1}/_{4}$" x $6^{1}/_{4}$"
QUILT SIZE: 42" x 55"

YARDAGE REQUIREMENTS

Yardage is based on 45"w fabric.

$2^{1}/_{4}$ yds of blue check
$^{1}/_{2}$ yd of white solid
scraps of primary colors for train appliqué
$2^{7}/_{8}$ yds for backing
$^{3}/_{4}$ yd for binding
45" x 60" batting

You will also need:
paper-backed fusible web
transparent monofilament thread for appliqué

CUTTING OUT THE PIECES

All measurements include a $^{1}/_{4}$" seam allowance. Follow ***Rotary Cutting****, page 41, to cut fabric.*

1. **From blue check:**
   - Cut 2 lengthwise strips $5^{1}/_{2}$" x 46" for **side borders**.
   - Cut 2 lengthwise strips $5^{1}/_{2}$" x 34" for **top/bottom borders**.
   - Cut 6 strips $6^{3}/_{4}$"w x remaining fabric width. From these strips, cut a total of 17 **squares** $6^{3}/_{4}$" x $6^{3}/_{4}$".
   - Cut 6 **strips** $1^{3}/_{4}$"w.
   - Cut 2 **strips** 3"w.
   - Cut 2 **strips** 3"w. From these strips, cut a total of 36 **rectangles** $1^{3}/_{4}$" x 3".
   - Cut 1 strip $5^{1}/_{2}$" x 22". From this strip, cut 4 **border squares** $5^{1}/_{2}$" x $5^{1}/_{2}$".
2. **From white solid:**
   - Cut 7 **strips** $1^{3}/_{4}$"w.
3. **From scraps:**
   - Use patterns, pages 37 and 38, and follow **Preparing Fusible Appliqués**, page 45, to cut the following number of appliqué pieces:

A — 4	I — 6	Q — 8
B — 4	J — 6	R — 4
C — 4	K — 30	S — 4
D — 4	L — 6	T — 8
E — 4	M — 4	U — 8
F — 4	N — 4	V — 4
G — 4	O —	
H — 48	P — 8	

ASSEMBLING THE QUILT TOP

Follow ***Piecing and Pressing****, page 43, to make quilt top.*

1. Sew $1^{3}/_{4}$"w **strips** together as shown to make **Strip Set A**. Make 6 **Strip Set A's**. Cut across **Strip Set A's** at $1^{3}/_{4}$" intervals to make 144 **Unit 1's**.

Strip Set A (make 6)

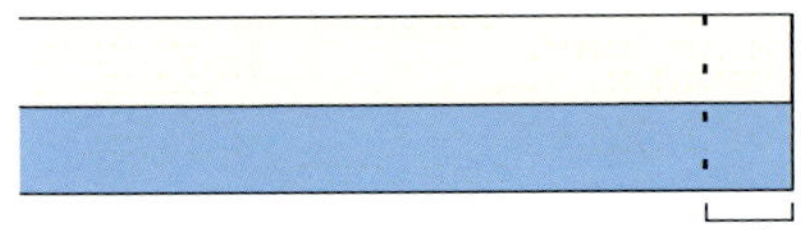

Unit 1 (make 144)

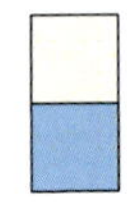

2. Sew 2 **Unit 1's** together to make **Unit 2**. Make 72 **Unit 2's**.

Unit 2 (make 72)

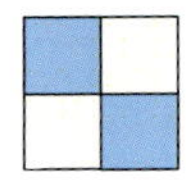

3. Sew 2 **Unit 2's** and 1 **rectangle** together to make **Unit 3**. Make 36 **Unit 3's**.

Unit 3 (make 36)

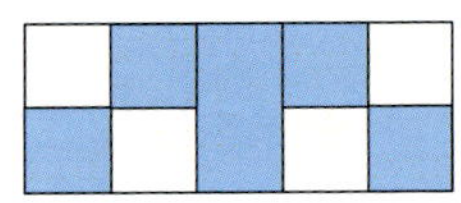

4. Sew **strips** together to make **Strip Set B**. Cut across **Strip Set B** at $1^{3}/_{4}$" intervals to make 18 **Unit 4's**.

Strip Set B (make 1)

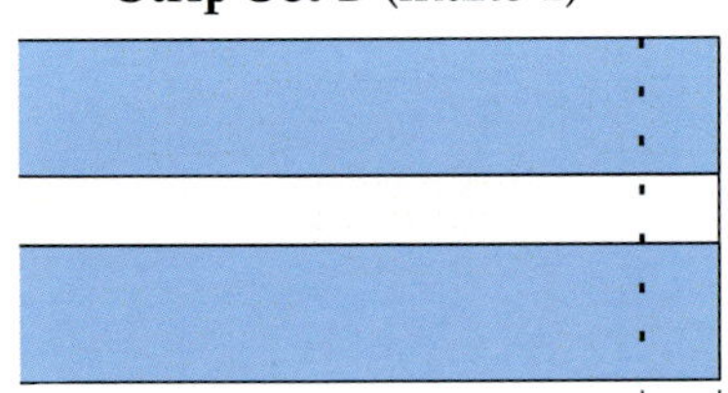

Unit 4 (make 18)

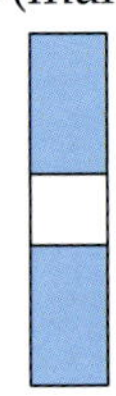

5. Sew 2 **Unit 3's** and 1 **Unit 4** together to make **Block**. Make 18 **Blocks**.

Block (make 18)

6. Referring to **Quilt Top Diagram**, sew **Blocks** and **squares** into rows; sew rows together to complete center section of quilt top.
7. For train border, follow **Invisible Appliqué**, page 45, and **Quilt Top Diagram** to appliqué pieces to **top/bottom borders**, **side borders**, and **border squares**.
8. Sew 1 **border square** to each end of each **side border.** Sew **top**, **bottom**, then **side borders** to center section to complete **Quilt Top**.

COMPLETING THE QUILT

1. Follow **Quilting**, page 47, to mark, layer, and quilt, using **Quilting Diagram** as a suggestion.
2. Cut a 27" square of binding fabric. Following **Binding**, page 49, to bind quilt using $2^1/_2$"w bias binding with mitered corners.

Quilting Diagram

Quilt Top Diagram

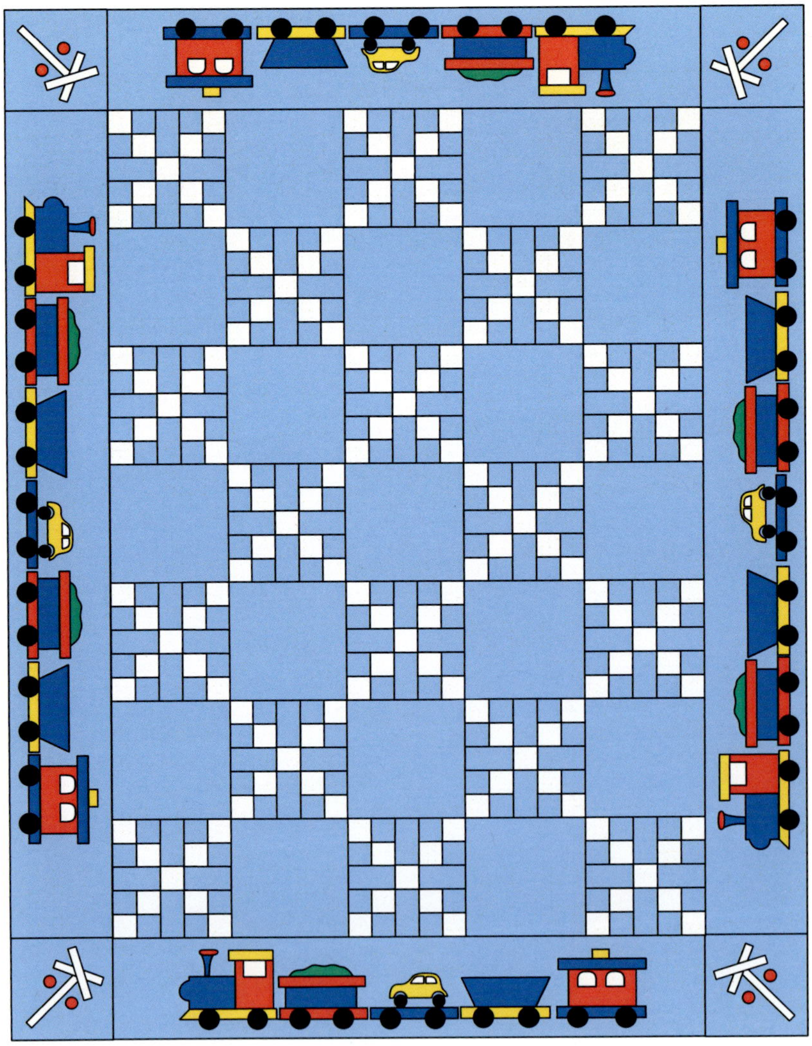

BUMPER PADS

Our bumper pads fit a standard (27" x 52") baby bed.

YARDAGE REQUIREMENTS

Yardage is based on 45"w fabric.

- $2^{1}/_{4}$ yds of blue check
- 3 yds of white solid
- $^{1}/_{2}$ yd scraps of primary colors for train appliqués
- $2^{1}/_{4}$ yds of 72"w upholstery batting
- 8 yds of $^{1}/_{4}$"w white double-fold bias tape

You will also need:

- transparent monofilament thread for appliqué
- paper-backed fusible web
- $19^{1}/_{2}$" x 28" piece of paper (newsprint or craft paper)
- 17 yds jumbo rickrack

CUTTING OUT THE PIECES

*Follow **Rotary Cutting**, page 41, to cut the following pieces, piecing as necessary to obtain indicated lengths.*

1. From white solid, cut 4 **side panels** 8" x 53", 2 **foot panels** 8" x 28", and 2 **rectangles** 20" x 29".
2. From blue check, cut 8 **side strips** $2^{1}/_{2}$" x 53", 4 **foot strips** $2^{1}/_{2}$" x 28", 2 **head strips** $2^{1}/_{2}$" x 28", and 2 **rectangles** 14" x 29".
3. Use patterns, pages 37 and 38, and follow **Preparing Fusible Appliqués**, page 45, to cut the following number of appliqué pieces from scraps:

A — 8	**I** — 12	**Q** — 16
B — 8	**J** — 12	**R** — 8
C — 8	**K** — 60	**S** — 8
D — 8	**L** — 12	
E — 8	**M** — 8	
F — 8	**N** — 8	
G — 8	**O** — 8	
H — 96	**P** — 16	

MAKING THE BUMPER PADS

*Follow **Piecing and Pressing**, page 43, to make bumper pads.*

1. To make head panel pattern, refer to **Fig. 1** to fold paper in half, matching short edges. Mark a point on short edge of paper 10" from bottom. Beginning at top of fold, draw a gentle freehand curve to marked point. Cut through both layers of paper and unfold.

Fig. 1

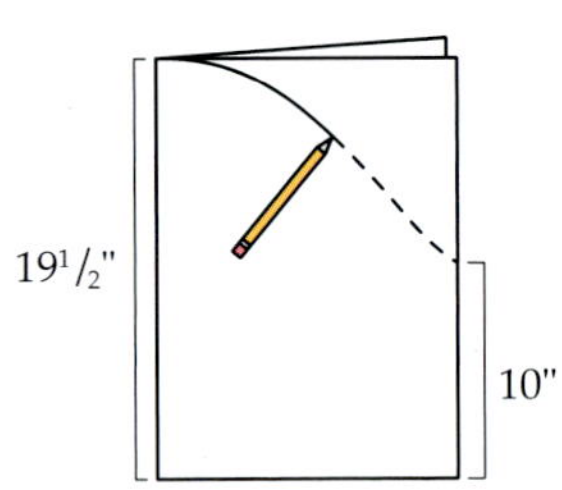

2. Use pattern to cut 2 **head panels** from white solid **rectangles**.
3. To make pattern for head panel trim, refer to **Fig. 2** to mark a line $2^{1}/_{4}$" from top edge of head panel pattern. Cut along marked line and discard lower portion.

Fig. 2

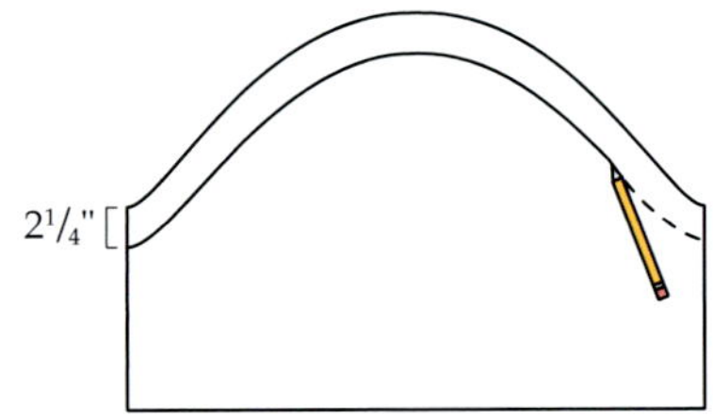

4. Use pattern to cut 2 **head panel trims** from blue check **rectangles**.
5. (***Note:*** Refer to panel diagrams, this page and page 37, for Steps 5 - 9.) Matching raw edges, baste wrong side of 1 **head panel trim** to right side of each **head panel**. Sew 1 **head strip** to bottom edge of each **head panel**.
6. Use head panel to cut 2 batting pieces.
7. Sew 1 **foot strip** each to top and bottom edges of each **foot panel**. Sew 1 **side strip** to top and bottom edges of each **side panel**.
8. Sew rickrack to **head**, **side**, and **foot panels**.
9. Follow **Invisible Appliqué**, page 45, to stitch **appliqués** to each **panel**.
10. Follow Steps 9-14 of **Nursery Rhyme Bumper Pads**, page 6, to complete pads.

Head Panel (make 2)

Foot Panel (make 2)

Side Panel (make 4)

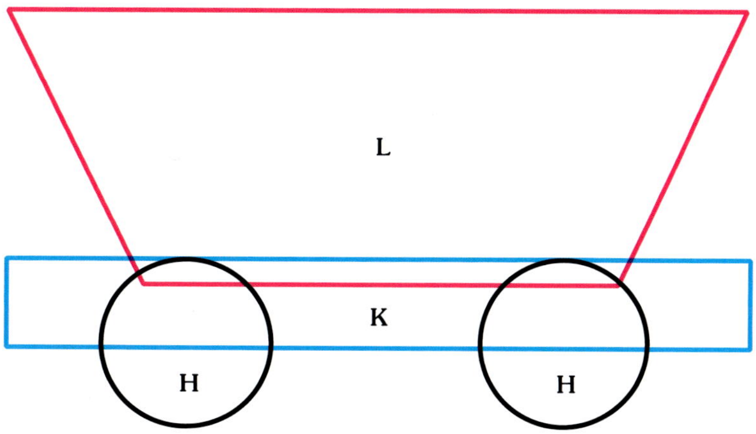

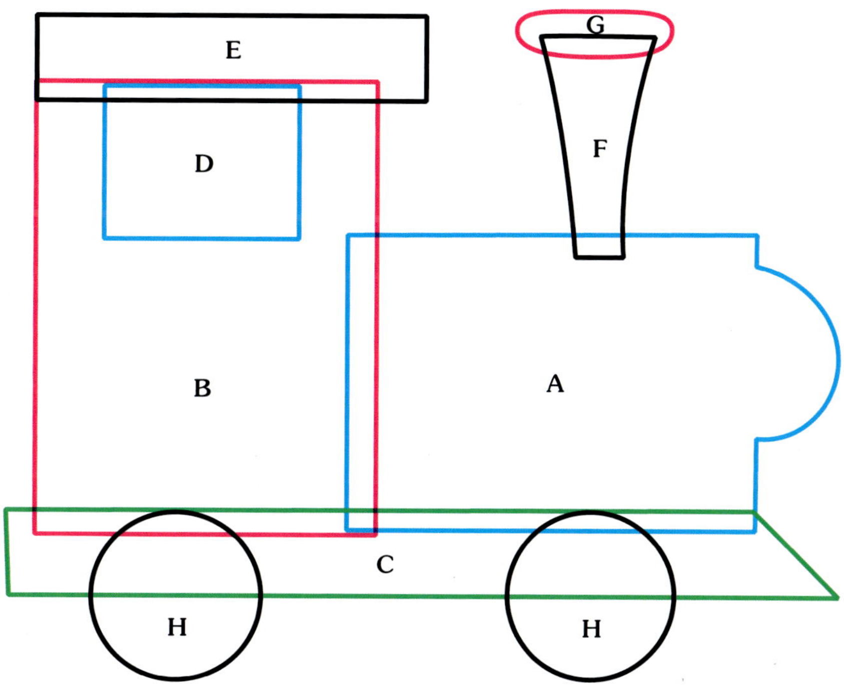

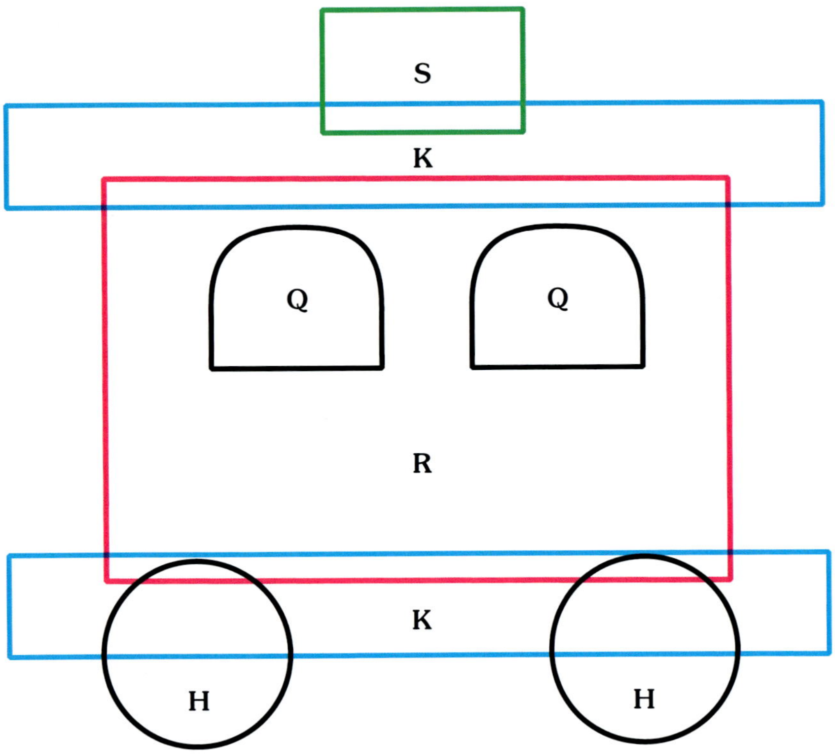
S
K
Q
Q
R
K
H
H

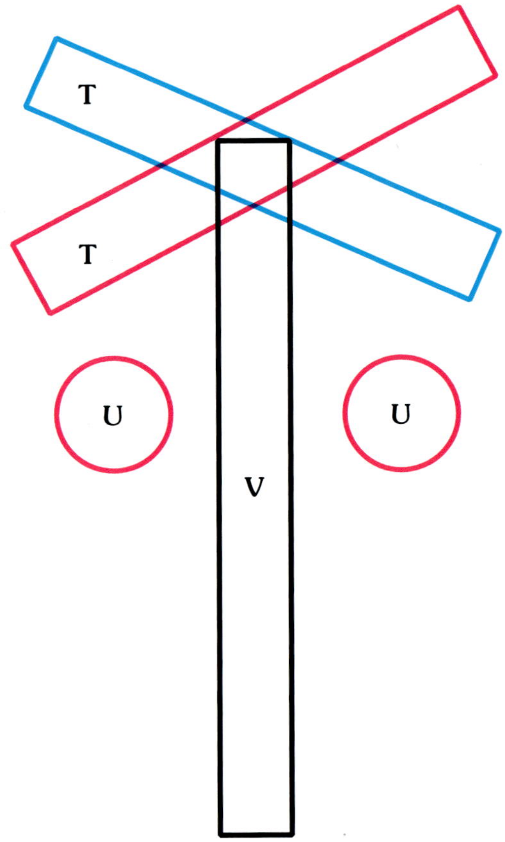
T
T
U
U
V

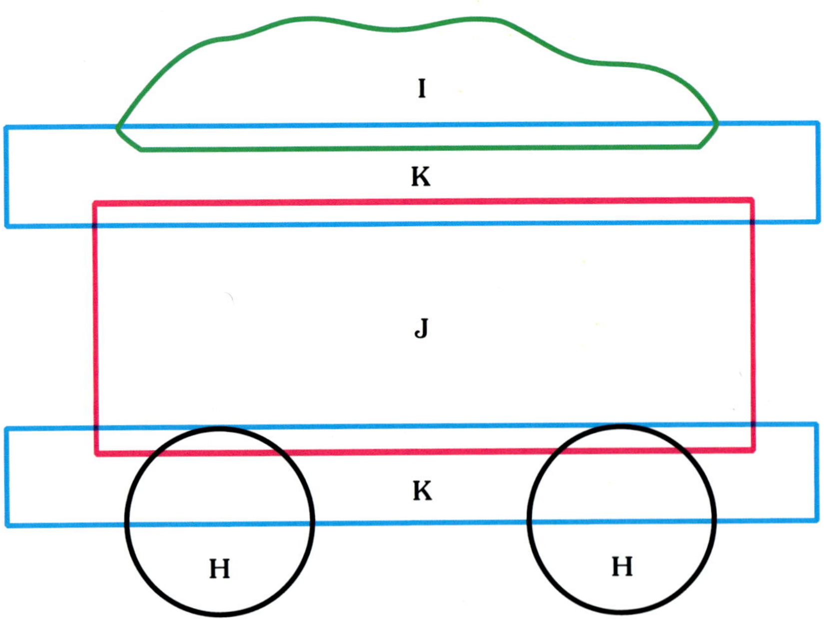
I
K
J
K
H
H

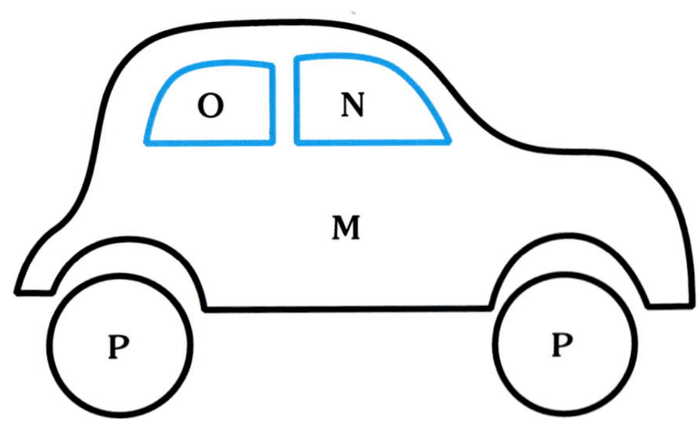
O
N
M
P
P

GENERAL INSTRUCTIONS

Complete instructions are given for making each of the wall hangings, quilts, and bumper pads shown in this book. To make your quilting easier and more enjoyable, we encourage you to carefully read all of these general instructions, study the color photographs, and familiarize yourself with the individual project instructions before beginning a project.

QUILTING SUPPLIES

This list includes all the tools you need for basic *quick-method quiltmaking*, plus additional supplies used for special techniques. Unless otherwise specified, all items may be found in your favorite fabric store or quilt shop.

Batting — Batting is most commonly available in polyester, cotton, or a polyester/cotton blend (see **Batting**, page 48).

Cutting mat — A cutting mat is a special mat designed to be used with a rotary cutter. A mat that measures approximately 18" x 24" is a good size for most cutting.

Eraser — A soft white fabric eraser or white art eraser may be used to remove pencil marks from fabric. Do not use a colored eraser, as the dye may discolor fabric.

Iron — An iron with both steam and dry settings and a smooth, clean soleplate is necessary for proper pressing.

Marking tools — There are many different types of marking tools available (see **Marking Quilting Lines**, page 47). A silver quilter's pencil is a good marker for both light and dark fabrics.

Masking tape — Two widths of masking tape, 1"w and 1/4"w, are helpful to have when quilting. The 1"w tape is used to secure the backing fabric to a flat surface when layering the quilt. The 1/4"w tape may be used as a guide when outline quilting.

Needles — Two types of needles are used for hand sewing: *Betweens*, used for quilting, are short and strong for stitching through layered fabric and batting. *Sharps* are longer, thinner needles used for basting and other hand sewing. For sewing machine needles, we recommend size 10 to 14 or 70 to 90 universal (sharp-pointed) needles.

Paper-backed fusible web — This iron-on adhesive with paper backing is used to secure fabric cutouts to another fabric when appliquéing. If the cutouts will be stitched in place, purchase the lighter weight web that will not gum up your sewing machine. A heavier weight web is used for appliqués that are fused in place with no stitching.

Permanent fine-point marker — A permanent marker is used to mark templates and stencils and to sign and date quilts. Test marker on fabric to make sure it will not bleed or wash out.

Pins — Straight pins made especially for quilting are extra long with large, round heads. Glass head pins will stand up to occasional contact with a hot iron. Some quilters prefer extra-fine dressmaker's silk pins.

Quilting hoop or frame — Quilting hoops and frames are designed to securely hold the 3 layers of a quilt together while you quilt. Many different types and sizes are available, including round and oval wooden hoops, frames made of rigid plastic pipe, and large floor frames made of either material. A 14" or 16" hoop allows you to quilt in your lap and makes your quilting portable.

Rotary cutter — The rotary cutter is the essential tool for quick-method quilting techniques. The cutter consists of a round, sharp blade mounted on a handle with a retractable blade guard for safety. It should be used only with a cutting mat and rotary cutting ruler. Two sizes are generally available; we recommend the larger (45 mm) size.

Rotary cutting rulers — A rotary cutting ruler is a thick, clear acrylic ruler made specifically for use with a rotary cutter. It should have accurate 1/8" crosswise and lengthwise markings and markings for 45° and 60° angles. A 6" x 24" ruler is a good size for most cutting. An additional 6" x 12" ruler or 12 1/2" square ruler is helpful when cutting wider pieces. Many specialty rulers are available that make specific cutting tasks faster and easier.

Scissors — Although most cutting will be done with a rotary cutter, sharp, high-quality scissors are still needed for some cutting. A separate pair of scissors for cutting paper and plastic is recommended. Smaller scissors are handy for clipping threads.

Seam ripper — A good seam ripper with a fine point is useful for removing stitching.

Sewing machine — A sewing machine that produces a good, even straight stitch is all that is necessary for most quilting. Zigzag stitch capability is necessary for Invisible Appliqué. Blindstitch with variable stitch width capability is required for Mock Hand Appliqué. Clean and oil your machine often and keep the tension set properly.

Stabilizer — Commercially made non-woven material or paper stabilizer is placed behind background fabric when doing Invisible Appliqué to provide a more stable stitching surface.

Template material — Sheets of translucent plastic, often pre-marked with a grid, are made especially for making templates.

Thimble — A thimble is necessary when hand quilting. Thimbles are available in metal, plastic, or leather and in many sizes and styles. Choose a thimble that fits well and is comfortable.

Thread — Several types of thread are used for quiltmaking: *General-purpose sewing thread* is used for basting, piecing, and some appliquéing. Buy high-quality cotton or cotton-covered polyester thread in light and dark neutrals, such as ecru and gray, for your basic supplies. *Quilting thread* is stronger than general-purpose sewing thread, and some brands have a coating to make them slide more easily through the quilt layers. Some machine appliqué projects in this book use *transparent monofilament (clear nylon) thread.* Use a very fine (.004 mm), soft nylon thread that is not stiff or wiry. Choose clear nylon thread for white or light fabrics or smoke nylon thread for darker fabrics.

Triangle — A large plastic right-angle triangle (available in art and office supply stores) is useful in rotary cutting for making first cuts to "square up" raw edges of fabric and for checking to see that cuts remain at right angles to the fold.

FABRICS

SELECTING FABRICS

For many quilters, choosing fabrics for a new project is one of the most fun, yet most challenging, parts of quiltmaking. Photographs of our quilts are excellent guides for choosing the colors for your project. You may choose to duplicate the colors in the photograph, or you may use the same light, medium, and dark values in completely different color families. When you change the light and dark value placement in a block, you may come up with a surprising new creation. The most important lesson to learn about fabrics and color is to choose fabrics you love. When you combine several fabrics you are simply crazy about in a quilt, you are sure to be happy with the results!

The yardage requirements listed for each project are based on 45" wide fabric with a "usable" width of 42" after shrinkage and trimming selvages. Your actual usable width will probably vary slightly from fabric to fabric. Though most fabrics will yield 42" or more, if you find a fabric that you suspect will yield a narrower usable width you will need to purchase additional yardage to compensate. Our recommended yardage lengths should be adequate for occasional resquaring of fabric when many cuts are required, but it never hurts to buy a little more fabric for insurance against a narrower usable width, the occasional cutting error, or to have on hand for making coordinating projects.

Choose high-quality, medium-weight, 100% cotton fabrics such as broadcloth or calico. All-cotton fabrics hold a crease better, fray less, and are easier to quilt than cotton/polyester blends. All the fabrics for a quilt should be of comparable weight and weave. Check the end of the fabric bolt for fiber content and width.

PREPARING FABRICS

All fabrics should be washed, dried, and pressed before cutting.

1. To check colorfastness before washing, cut a small piece of the fabric and place in a glass of hot water with a little detergent. Leave fabric in the water for a few minutes. Remove from water and blot fabric with white paper towels. If any color bleeds onto the towels, wash the fabric separately with warm water and detergent, then rinse until the water runs clear. If fabric continues to bleed, choose another fabric.
2. Unfold yardage and separate fabrics by color. To help reduce raveling, use scissors to snip a small triangle from each corner of your fabric pieces. Machine wash fabrics in warm water with a small amount of mild laundry detergent. Do not use fabric softener. Rinse well and then dry fabrics in the dryer, checking long fabric lengths occasionally to make sure they are not tangling.
3. To make ironing easier, remove fabrics from dryer while they are slightly damp. Refold each fabric lengthwise (as it was on the bolt) with wrong sides together and matching selvages. If necessary, adjust slightly at selvages so that fold lies flat. Press each fabric with a steam iron set on "Cotton."

ROTARY CUTTING

Based on the idea that you can easily cut strips of fabric and then cut those strips into smaller pieces, rotary cutting has brought speed and accuracy to quiltmaking. Observe safety precautions when using the rotary cutter since it is extremely sharp. Develop a habit of retracting the blade guard just before making a cut and closing it immediately afterward, before laying down the cutter.

1. Follow **Preparing Fabrics** to wash, dry, and press fabrics.
2. Cut all strips from the selvage-to-selvage width of the fabric unless otherwise indicated. Place fabric on the cutting mat as shown in **Fig. 1** with the fold of the fabric toward you. To straighten the uneven fabric edge, make the first "squaring up" cut by placing the right edge of the rotary cutting ruler over the left raw edge of the fabric. Place right-angle triangle (or another rotary cutting ruler) with the lower edge carefully aligned with the fold and the left edge against the ruler (**Fig. 1**). Hold the ruler firmly with your left hand, placing your little finger off the left edge to anchor the ruler. Remove the triangle, pick up the rotary cutter, and retract the blade guard. Using a smooth, downward motion, make the cut by running the blade of the rotary cutter firmly along the right edge of the ruler (**Fig. 2**). Always cut in a direction away from your body and immediately close the blade guard after each cut.

Fig. 1

Fig. 2

3. To cut each of the strips required for the project, place the ruler over the cut edge of the fabric, aligning desired marking on the ruler with the cut edge (**Fig. 3**) and then make the cut. When cutting several strips from a single piece of fabric, it is important to occasionally use the ruler and triangle to ensure that cuts are still at a perfect right angle to the fold. If not, repeat Step 2 to straighten.

Fig. 3

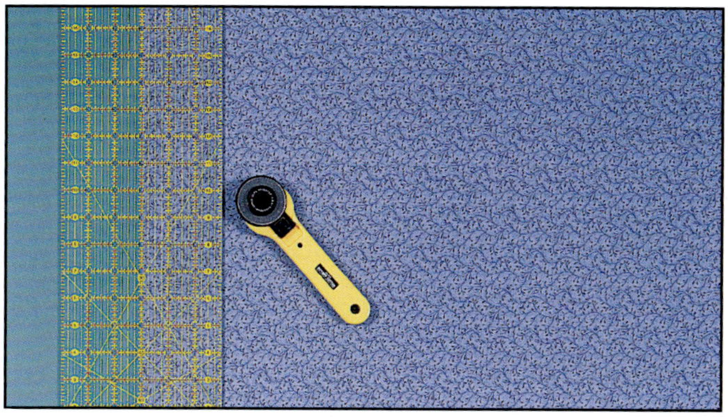

4. To square up selvage ends of a strip before cutting pieces, refer to **Fig. 4** and place folded strip on mat with selvage ends to your right. Aligning a horizontal marking on ruler with 1 long edge of strip, use rotary cutter to trim off selvage to make end of strip square and even (**Fig. 4**). Turn strip (or entire mat) so that cut end is to your left before making subsequent cuts.

Fig. 4

5. Pieces such as rectangles and squares can now be cut from strips. Usually strips remain folded, and pieces are cut in pairs after ends of strips are squared up. To cut squares or rectangles from a strip, place ruler over left end of strip, aligning desired marking on ruler with cut end of strip. To ensure perfectly square cuts, align a horizontal marking on ruler with 1 long edge of strip (**Fig. 5**) before making the cut.

Fig. 5

6. To cut 2 triangles from a square, cut square the size indicated in the project instructions. Cut square once diagonally to make 2 triangles (**Fig. 6**).

Fig. 6

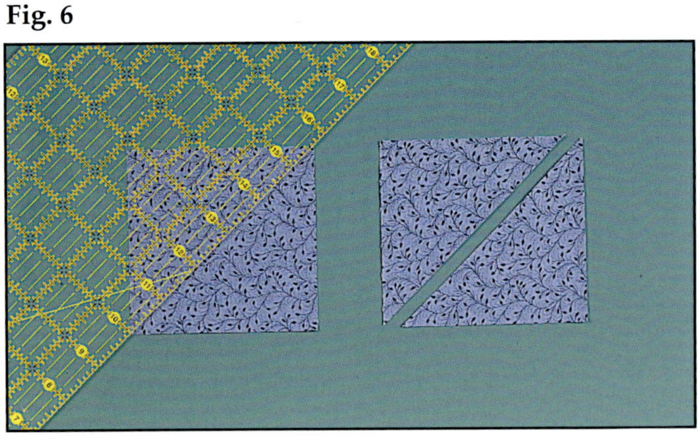

7. To cut 4 triangles from a square, cut square the size indicated in the project instructions. Cut square twice diagonally to make 4 triangles (**Fig. 7**). You may find it helpful to use a small rotary cutting mat so that mat can be turned to make second cut without disturbing fabric pieces.

Fig. 7

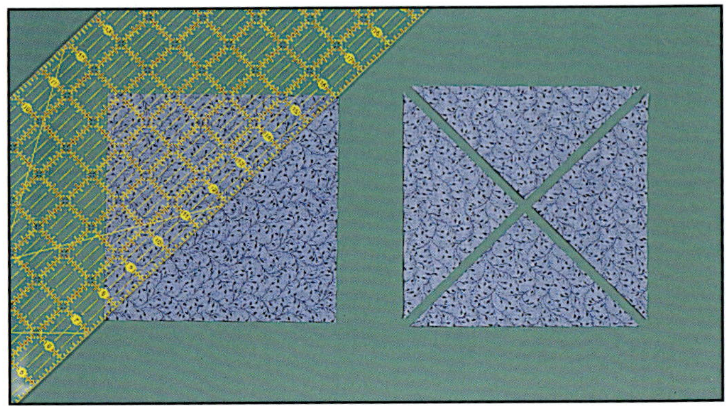

8. After some practice, you may want to try stacking up to 6 fabric layers when making cuts. When stacking strips, match long cut edges and follow Step 4 to square up ends of strip stack. Carefully turn stack (or entire mat) so that squared-up ends are to your left before making subsequent cuts. After cutting, check accuracy of pieces.
9. In some cases, strips will be sewn together into strip sets before being cut into smaller units. When cutting a strip set, align a seam in strip set with a horizontal marking on the ruler to maintain square cuts (**Fig. 8**). We do not recommend stacking strip sets for rotary cutting.

Fig. 8

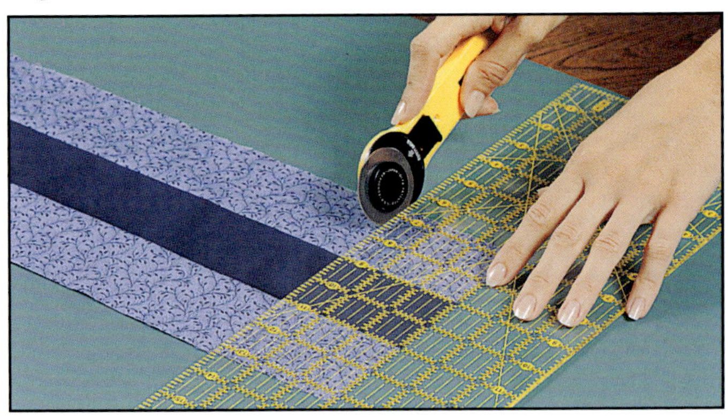

10. Occasionally, you will need to cut strips along the length of a fabric. To remove selvages before cutting lengthwise strips, place fabric on mat with selvages to your left and squared-up end at bottom of mat. Placing ruler over selvage and using squared-up edge instead of fold, follow Step 2 to cut away selvages as you did raw edges (**Fig. 9**). After making a cut the length of the mat, move the next section of fabric to be cut onto the mat. Repeat until you have removed selvages from required length of fabric.

Fig. 9

11. After removing selvages, place ruler over left edge of fabric, aligning desired marking on ruler with cut edge of fabric. Make cuts as in Step 3. After each cut, move next section of fabric onto mat as in Step 10.

TEMPLATE CUTTING

Our full-sized piecing templates have 2 lines: a solid cutting line and a dashed line showing the 1/4" seam allowance.

1. To make a template from a pattern, use a permanent fine-point marker to carefully trace pattern onto template plastic, making sure to transfer all alignment and grain line markings. Cut out template along inner edge of drawn line. Check template against original pattern for accuracy.
2. To use a template, place template on wrong side of fabric (unless indicated otherwise), aligning grain line on template with straight grain of fabric. Use a sharp fabric marking pencil to draw around template. Transfer all alignment markings to fabric. Cut out fabric piece using scissors or rotary cutter and ruler.

PIECING AND PRESSING

Precise cutting, followed by accurate piecing and careful pressing, will ensure that all the pieces of your quilt top fit together well.

PIECING

Set sewing machine stitch length for approximately 11 stitches per inch. Use a new, sharp needle suited for medium-weight woven fabric.

Use a neutral-colored general-purpose sewing thread (not quilting thread) in the needle and in the bobbin. Stitch first on a scrap of fabric to check upper and bobbin thread tension; make any adjustments necessary.

For good results, it is essential that you stitch with an accurate 1/4" seam allowance. On many sewing machines, the measurement from the needle to the outer edge of the presser foot is 1/4". If this is the case with your machine, the presser foot is your best guide. If not, measure 1/4" from the needle and mark with a piece of masking tape. Special presser feet that are exactly 1/4" wide are also available for most sewing machines.

When piecing, always place pieces right sides together and match raw edges; pin if necessary. (If using straight pins, remove the pins just before they reach the sewing machine needle.)

Chain Piecing

Chain piecing whenever possible will make your work go faster and will usually result in more accurate piecing. Stack the pieces you will be sewing beside your machine in the order you will need them and in a position that will allow you to easily pick them up. Pick up each pair of pieces, carefully place them together as they will be sewn, and feed them into the machine one after the other. Stop between each pair only long enough to pick up the next and don't cut thread between pairs (**Fig. 10**). After all pieces are sewn, cut threads, press, and go on to the next step, chain piecing when possible.

Fig. 10

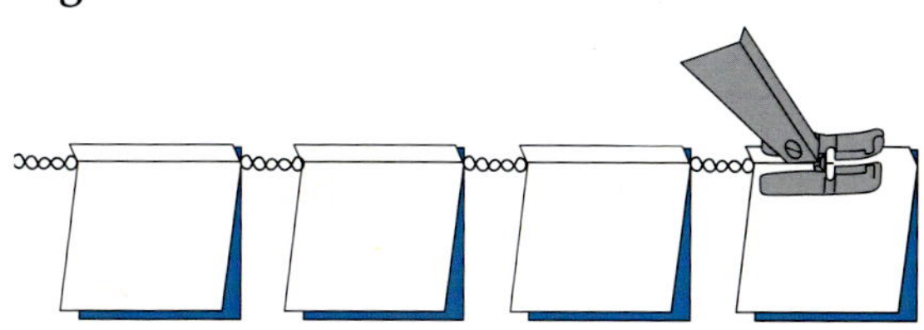

Sewing Strip Sets

When there are several strips to assemble into a strip set, first sew the strips together into pairs, then sew the pairs together to form the strip set. To help avoid distortion, sew 1 seam in 1 direction and then sew the next seam in the opposite direction (**Fig. 11**).

Fig. 11

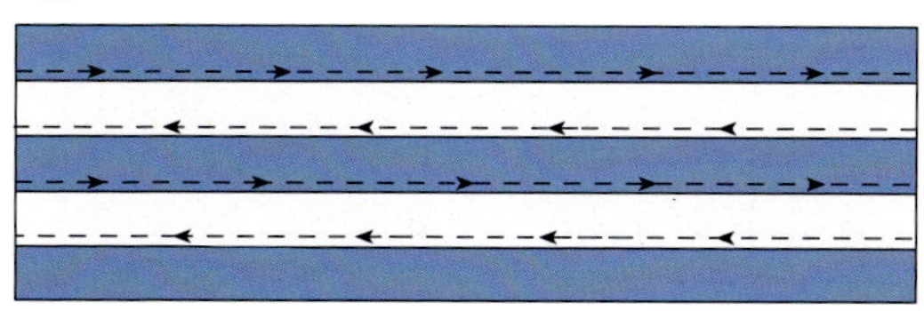

Sewing Across Seam Intersections

When sewing across the intersection of 2 seams, place pieces right sides together and match seams exactly, making sure seam allowances are pressed in opposite directions (**Fig. 12**). To prevent fabric from shifting, you may wish to pin in place.

Fig. 12

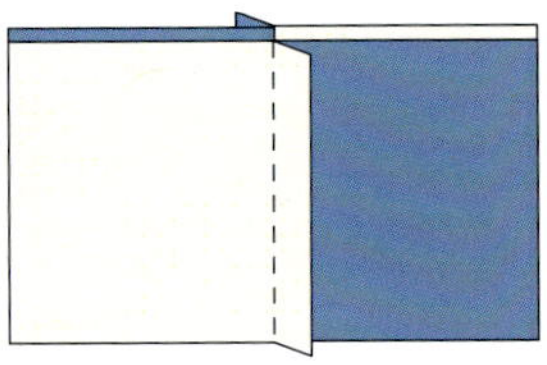

Sewing Sharp Points

To ensure sharp points when joining triangular or diagonal pieces, stitch across the center of the "X" (shown in pink) formed on the wrong side by previous seams (**Fig. 13**).

Fig. 13

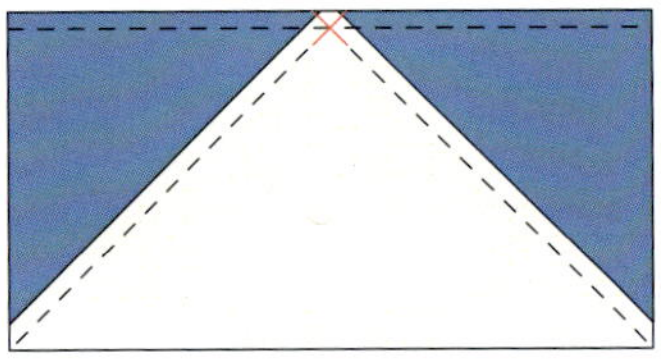

Sewing Bias Seams

Care should be used in handling and stitching bias edges, since they stretch easily. After sewing the seam, carefully press seam allowances to 1 side, making sure not to stretch the fabric.

Making Triangle-Squares

The grid method for making triangle-squares is faster and more accurate than cutting and sewing individual triangles. Stitching before cutting the triangle-squares apart also prevents stretching the bias edges.

1. Follow project instructions to cut rectangles or squares of fabric for making triangle-squares. Place the indicated pieces right sides together and press.
2. On the wrong side of the lighter fabric, draw a grid of squares similar to that shown in **Fig. 14**. The size and number of squares will be given in the project instructions.

Fig. 14

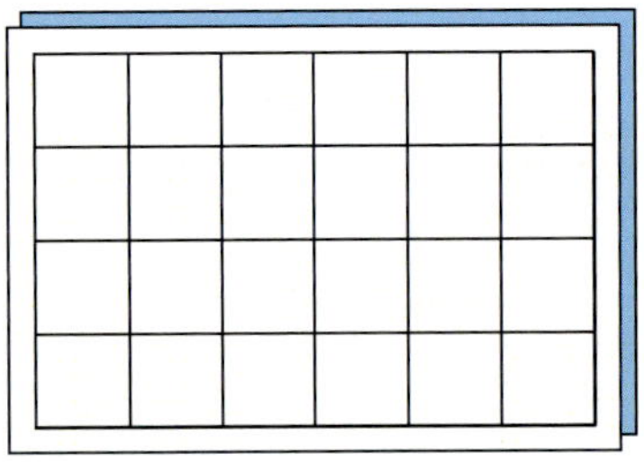

3. Following the example given in the project instructions, draw 1 diagonal line through each square in the grid (**Fig. 15**).

Fig. 15

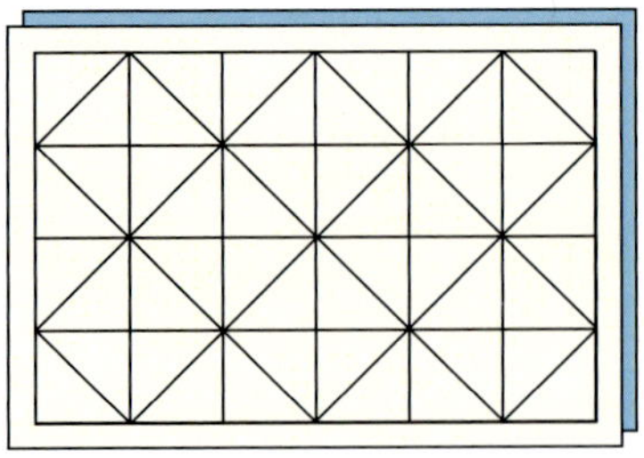

4. Stitch 1/4" on each side of all diagonal lines. For accuracy, it may be helpful to first draw your stitching lines onto the fabric, especially if your presser foot is not your 1/4" guide. In some cases, stitching may be done in a single continuous line. Project instructions include a diagram similar to **Fig. 16**, which shows stitching lines and the direction of the stitching.

Fig. 16

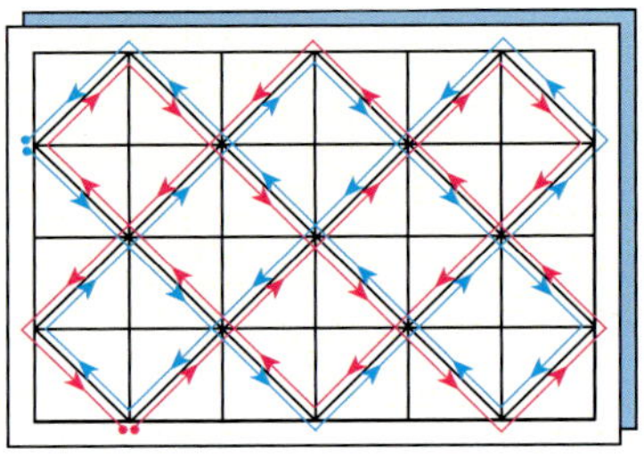

5. Use rotary cutter and ruler to cut along all drawn lines of the grid. Each square of the grid will yield 2 triangle-squares (**Fig. 17**).

Fig. 17

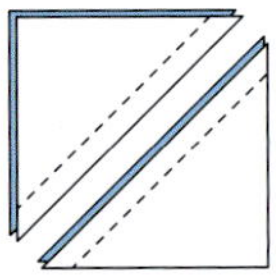

6. Carefully press triangle-squares open, pressing seam allowances toward darker fabric. Trim off points of seam allowances that extend beyond edges of triangle-square.

PRESSING

Use a steam iron set on "Cotton" for all pressing. Press as you sew, taking care to prevent small folds along seamlines. Seam allowances are almost always pressed to one side, usually toward the darker fabric. However, to reduce bulk it may occasionally be necessary to press seam allowances toward the lighter fabric or even to press them open. In order to prevent a dark fabric seam allowance from showing through a light fabric, trim the darker seam allowance slightly narrower than the lighter seam allowance. To press long seams, such as those in long strip sets, without curving or other distortion, lay strips across the width of the ironing board.

APPLIQUÉ

PREPARING FUSIBLE APPLIQUÉS

Patterns are printed in reverse to enable you to use our speedy method of preparing appliqués. White or light-colored fabrics may need to be lined with fusible interfacing before applying fusible web to prevent darker fabrics from showing through.

1. Place paper-backed fusible web, web side down, over appliqué pattern. Use a pencil to trace pattern onto paper side of web as many times as indicated in project instructions for a single fabric. Repeat for additional patterns and fabrics.
2. Follow manufacturer's instructions to fuse traced patterns to wrong side of fabrics. Do not remove paper backing.
3. Some projects may have pieces that are given as measurements (such as a 2" x 4" rectangle) instead of drawn patterns. Fuse web to wrong side of the fabrics indicated for these pieces.
4. Use scissors to cut out appliqué pieces along traced lines; use rotary cutting equipment to cut out appliqué pieces given as measurements. Remove paper backing from all pieces.

INVISIBLE APPLIQUÉ

This method of appliqué is an adaptation of satin stitch appliqué that uses clear nylon thread to secure the appliqué pieces. Transparent monofilament (clear nylon) thread is available in 2 colors: clear and smoke. Use clear on white or very light fabrics and smoke on darker colors.

1. Referring to diagram and/or photo, arrange appliqués on the background fabric and follow manufacturer's instructions to fuse in place.
2. Pin a stabilizer, such as paper or any of the commercially available products, on wrong side of background fabric before stitching appliqués in place.
3. Thread sewing machine with transparent monofilament thread; use general-purpose thread that matches background fabric in bobbin.
4. Set sewing machine for a very narrow (approximately $^{1}/_{16}$") zigzag stitch and a short stitch length. You may find that loosening the top tension slightly will yield a smoother stitch.
5. Begin by stitching 2 or 3 stitches in place (drop feed dogs or set stitch length at 0) to anchor thread. Most of the zigzag stitch should be done on the appliqué with the right edges of the stitch falling at the very outside edge of the appliqué. Stitch over all exposed raw edges of appliqué pieces.
6. (*Note:* Dots on **Figs. 18-23** indicate where to leave needle in fabric when pivoting.) For outside corners, stitch just past the corner, stopping with the needle in background fabric (**Fig. 18**). Raise presser foot. Pivot project, lower presser foot, and stitch adjacent side (**Fig. 19**).

Fig. 18

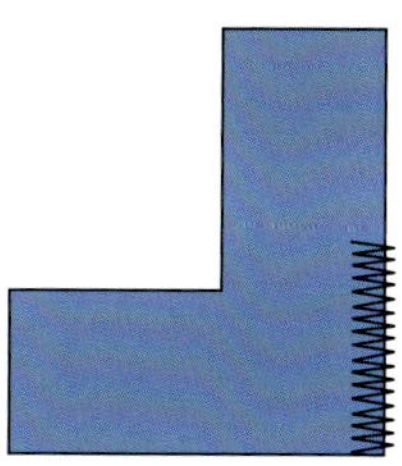

Fig. 19

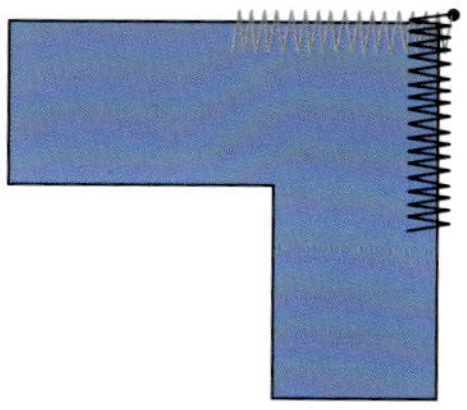

7. For inside corners, stitch just past the corner, stopping with the needle in appliqué fabric (**Fig. 20**). Raise presser foot. Pivot project, lower presser foot, and stitch adjacent side (**Fig. 21**).

Fig. 20

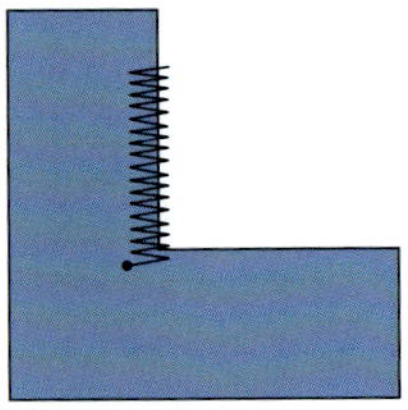

Fig. 21

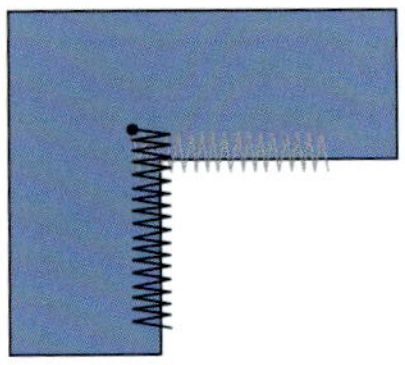

8. When stitching outside curves, stop with needle in background fabric. Raise presser foot and pivot project as needed. Lower presser foot and continue stitching, pivoting as often as necessary to follow curve (**Fig. 22**).

Fig. 22

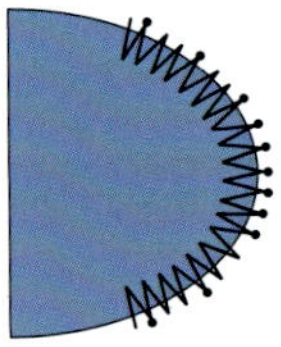

9. When stitching inside curves, stop with needle in appliqué fabric. Raise presser foot and pivot project as needed. Lower presser foot and continue stitching, pivoting as often as necessary to follow curve (**Fig. 23**).

Fig. 23

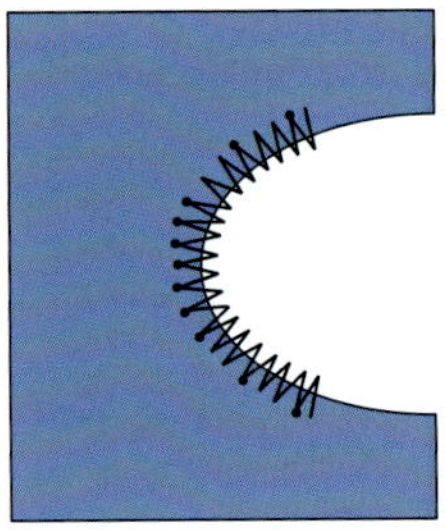

10. Do not backstitch at end of stitching. Pull threads to wrong side of background fabric; knot thread and trim ends.
11. Carefully tear away stabilizer.

MOCK HAND APPLIQUÉ

This technique uses the blindstitch on your sewing machine to achieve a look that closely resembles traditional hand appliqué. Using an updated method, appliqués are prepared with turned-under edges and then machine stitched to the background fabric. For best appliqué results, your sewing machine must have blindstitch capability with a variable stitch width. If your blindstitch width cannot be adjusted, you may still wish to try this technique to see if you are happy with the results. Some sewing machines have a narrower blindstitch width than others.

1. Follow project instructions to prepare appliqué pieces.
2. Thread needle of sewing machine with transparent monofilament thread; use general-purpose thread in bobbin in a color to match background fabric.
3. Set sewing machine for narrow blindstitch (just wide enough to catch 2 or 3 threads of the appliqué) and a very short stitch length (20 - 30 stitches per inch).
4. Arrange appliqué pieces on background fabric as described in project instructions. Use pins or hand baste to secure.
5. (***Note:*** Follow Steps 6 - 9 of **Invisible Appliqué**, page 45, for needle position when pivoting.) Sew around edges of each appliqué so that the straight stitches fall on the background fabric very near the appliqué and the "hem" stitches barely catch the folded edge of the appliqué (**Fig. 24**).

Fig. 24

6. It is not necessary to backstitch at the beginning or end of stitching. End stitching by sewing $^1/_4$" over the first stitches. Trim thread ends close to fabric.
7. To reduce bulk, turn project over and use scissors to cut away background fabric approximately $^1/_4$" inside stitching line of appliqué as shown in **Fig. 25**.

Fig. 25

QUILTING

Quilting holds the 3 layers (top, batting, and backing) of the quilt together. Our project instructions show you quilting diagrams that can be used as suggestions for marking quilting designs. Because marking, layering, and quilting are interrelated and may be done in different orders depending on circumstances, please read this entire section, pages 47 - 49, before beginning the quilting process on your project.

TYPES OF QUILTING

In the Ditch

Quilting very close to a seamline (**Fig. 26**) or appliqué (**Fig. 27**) is called "in the ditch" quilting. This type of quilting does not need to be marked and is indicated on our quilting diagrams with blue lines close to seamlines. When quilting in the ditch, quilt on the side opposite the seam allowance.

Fig. 26

Fig. 27

Outline Quilting

Quilting approximately $^1/_4$" from a seam or appliqué is called "outline" quilting (**Fig. 28**). This type of quilting is indicated on our quilting diagrams by blue lines a short distance from seamlines. Outline quilting may be marked, or you may place $^1/_4$"w masking tape along seamlines and quilt along the opposite edge of the tape. (Do not leave tape on quilt longer than necessary, since it may leave an adhesive residue.)

Fig. 28

Ornamental Quilting

Quilting decorative lines or designs is called "ornamental" quilting (**Fig. 29**). Ornamental quilting is indicated on our quilting diagrams by blue lines. This type of quilting should be marked before you baste quilt layers together.

Fig. 29

MARKING QUILTING LINES

Fabric marking pencils, various types of chalk markers, and fabric marking pens with inks that disappear with exposure to air or water are readily available and work well for different applications. Lead pencils work well on light-colored fabric, but marks may be difficult to remove. White pencils work well on dark-colored fabric, and silver pencils show up well on many colors. Since chalk rubs off easily, it's a good choice if you are marking as you quilt. Fabric marking pens make more durable and visible markings, but the marks should be carefully removed according to manufacturer's instructions. Press down only as hard as necessary to make a visible line.

When you choose to mark your quilt, whether before or after the layers are basted together, is also a factor in deciding which marking tool to use. If you mark with chalk or a chalk pencil, handling the quilt during basting may rub off the markings. Intricate or ornamental designs may not be practical to mark as you quilt; mark these designs before basting using a more durable marker.

To choose marking tools, take all these factors into consideration and test different markers on scrap fabric until you find the one that gives the desired result.

USING QUILTING STENCILS

A wide variety of pre-cut quilting stencils, as well as entire books of quilting patterns, are available at your local quilt shop or fabric store. Wherever you draw your quilting inspiration from, using a stencil makes it easier to mark intricate or repetitive designs on your quilt top.

1. To make a stencil from a pattern, center template plastic over pattern and use a permanent marker to trace pattern onto plastic.
2. Use a craft knife with a single or double blade to cut narrow slits along traced lines (**Fig. 30**).

Fig. 30

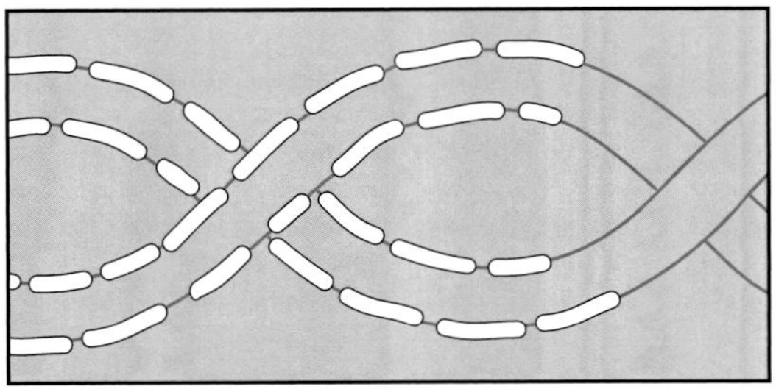

3. Use desired marking tool and stencil to mark quilting lines.

CHOOSING AND PREPARING THE BACKING AND BATTING

Backing

To allow for slight shifting of the quilt top during quilting, the backing should be approximately 2" larger on all sides.

1. Measure length and width of quilt top; add 4" to each measurement.
2. Cut backing fabric determined size, piecing if necessary.

Batting

Choosing the right batting will make your quilting job easier. For fine hand quilting, choose a low-loft batting in any of the fiber types described here.

Batting is available in many different fibers. Bonded polyester batting is one of the most popular batting types. It is treated with a protective coating to stabilize the fibers and to reduce "bearding," a process where batting fibers work their way out through the quilt fabrics. Other batting options include cotton/polyester batting, which combines the best of both polyester and cotton battings; all-cotton batting, which must be quilted more closely than polyester batting; and wool and silk battings, which are generally more expensive and are usually only dry-cleanable.

Whichever batting you choose, read the manufacturer's instructions closely for any special notes on care or preparation. When you're ready to use your chosen batting in a project, cut the batting the same size as the prepared backing.

LAYERING THE QUILT

1. Examine wrong side of quilt top closely; trim any seam allowances and clip any threads that may show through the front of the quilt. Press quilt top.
2. If quilt top is to be marked before layering, mark quilting lines (see **Marking Quilting Lines**, page 47).
3. Place backing wrong side up on a flat surface. Use masking tape to tape edges of backing to surface. Place batting on top of backing fabric. Smooth batting gently, being careful not to stretch or tear. Center quilt top right side up on batting.
4. If hand quilting, begin in the center and work toward the outer edges to hand baste all layers together. Use long stitches and place basting lines approximately 4" apart (**Fig. 31**). Smooth fullness or wrinkles toward outer edges.

Fig. 31

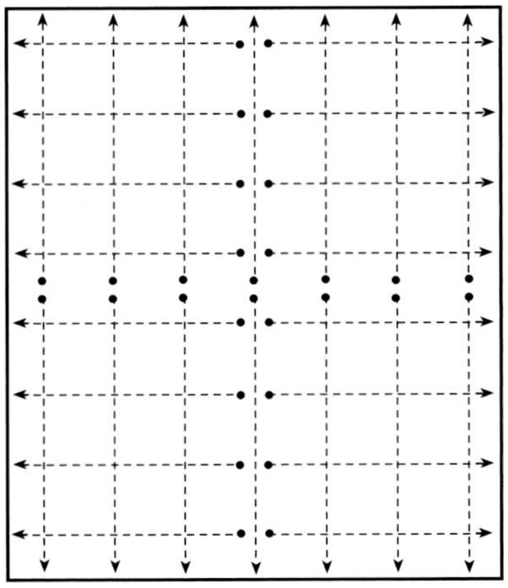

HAND QUILTING

The quilting stitch is a basic running stitch that forms a broken line on the quilt top and backing. Stitches on the quilt top and backing should be straight and equal in length.

1. Secure center of quilt in hoop or frame. Check quilt top and backing to make sure they are smooth. To help prevent puckers, always begin quilting in the center of the quilt and work toward the outside edges.
2. Thread needle with an 18" - 20" length of quilting thread; knot 1 end. Using a thimble, insert needle into quilt top and batting approximately $^1/_2$" from where you wish to begin quilting. Bring needle up at the point where you wish to begin (**Fig. 32**); when knot catches on quilt top, give thread a quick, short pull to "pop" knot through fabric into batting (**Fig. 33**).

Fig. 32

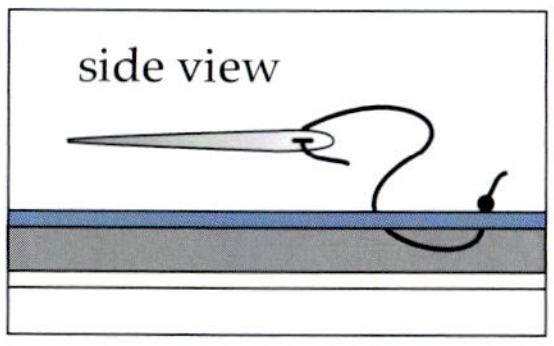

Fig. 33

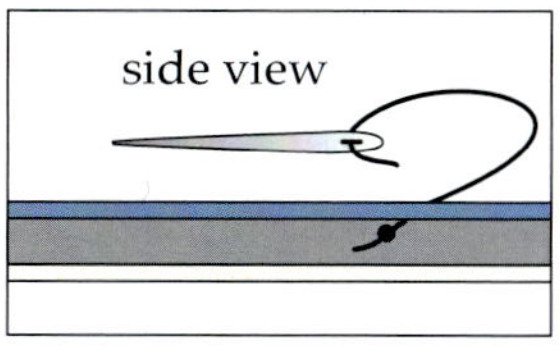

3. Holding the needle with your sewing hand and placing your other hand underneath the quilt, use thimble to push the tip of the needle down through all layers. As soon as needle touches your finger underneath, use that finger to push the tip of the needle only back up through the layers to top of quilt. (The amount of the needle showing above the fabric determines the length of the quilting stitch.) Referring to **Fig. 34**, rock the needle up and down, taking 3 - 6 stitches before bringing the needle and thread completely through the layers. Check the back of the quilt to make sure stitches are going through all layers. When quilting through a seam allowance or quilting a curve or corner, you may need to take 1 stitch at a time.

Fig. 34

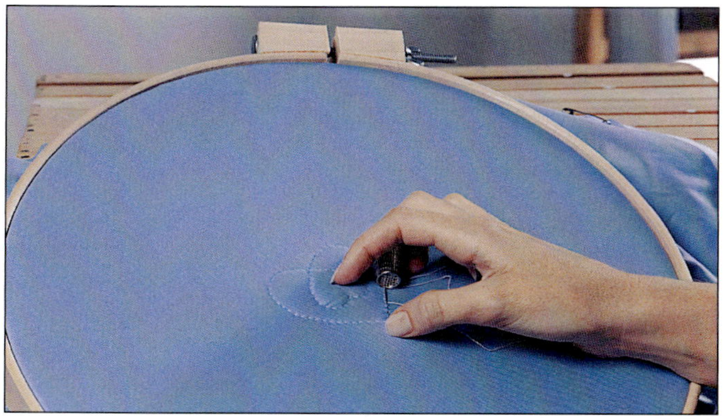

4. When you reach the end of your thread, knot thread close to the fabric and "pop" knot into batting; clip thread close to fabric.
5. Stop and move your hoop as often as necessary. You do not have to tie a knot every time you move your hoop; you may leave the thread dangling and pick it up again when you return to that part of the quilt.

BINDING

Binding encloses the raw edges of your quilt. Because of its stretchiness, bias binding works well for binding projects with curves or rounded corners and tends to lie smooth and flat in any given circumstance. It is also more durable than other types of binding. Binding may also be cut from the straight lengthwise or crosswise grain of the fabric. You will find that straight-grain binding works well for projects with straight edges.

MAKING CONTINUOUS BIAS STRIP BINDING

Bias strips for binding can simply be cut and pieced to the desired length. However, when a long length of binding is needed, the "continuous" method is quick and accurate.

1. Cut a square from binding fabric the size indicated in the project instructions. Cut square in half diagonally to make 2 triangles.
2. With right sides together and using a $^1/_4$" seam allowance, sew triangles together (**Fig. 35**); press seam allowance open.

Fig. 35

3. On wrong side of fabric, draw lines the width of the binding as specified in the project instructions (**Fig. 36**). Cut off any remaining fabric less than this width.

Fig. 36

4. With right sides inside, bring short edges together to form a tube; match raw edges so that first drawn line of top section meets second drawn line of bottom section (**Fig. 37**).

Fig. 37

5. Carefully pin edges together by inserting pins through drawn lines at the point where drawn lines intersect, making sure the pins go through intersections on both sides. Using a $^1/_4$" seam allowance, sew edges together. Press seam allowance open.
6. To cut continuous strip, begin cutting along first drawn line (**Fig. 38**). Continue cutting along drawn line around tube.

Fig. 38

7. Trim ends of bias strip square.
8. Matching wrong sides and raw edges, press bias strip in half lengthwise to complete binding.

MAKING STRAIGHT-GRAIN BINDING

1. To determine length of strip needed if attaching binding with mitered corners, measure edges of the quilt and add 12".
2. To determine lengths of strips needed if attaching binding with overlapped corners, measure each edge of quilt; add 3" to each measurement.
3. Cut lengthwise or crosswise strips of binding fabric the determined length and the width called for in the project instructions. Strips may be pieced to achieve the necessary length.
4. Matching wrong sides and raw edges, press strip(s) in half lengthwise to complete binding.

ATTACHING BINDING WITH MITERED CORNERS

1. Press 1 end of binding diagonally (**Fig. 39**).

Fig. 39

2. Lay binding around quilt to make sure that seams in binding will not end up at a corner. Adjust placement if necessary. Matching raw edges of binding to raw edge of quilt top and beginning with pressed end several inches from a corner, pin binding to right side of quilt along 1 edge.
3. When you reach the first corner, mark $^1/_4$" from corner of quilt top (**Fig. 40**).

Fig. 40

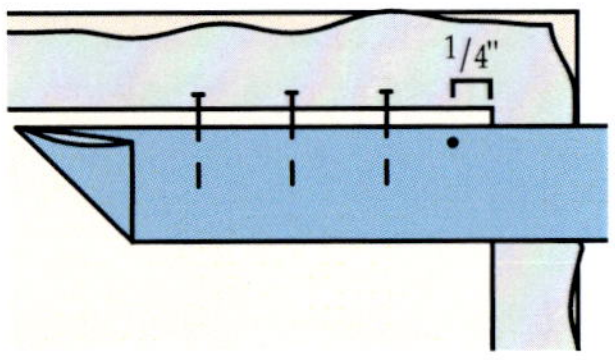

4. Using a $^1/_4$" seam allowance, sew binding to quilt, backstitching at beginning of stitching and when you reach the mark (**Fig. 41**). Lift needle out of fabric and clip thread.

Fig. 41

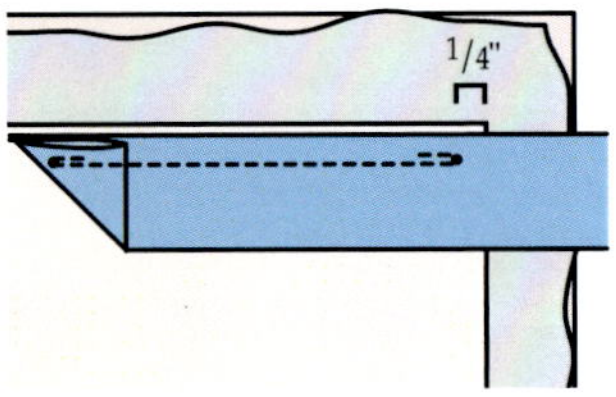

5. Fold binding as shown in **Figs. 42** and **43** and pin binding to adjacent side, matching raw edges. When you reach the next corner, mark $^1/_4$" from edge of quilt top.

Fig. 42

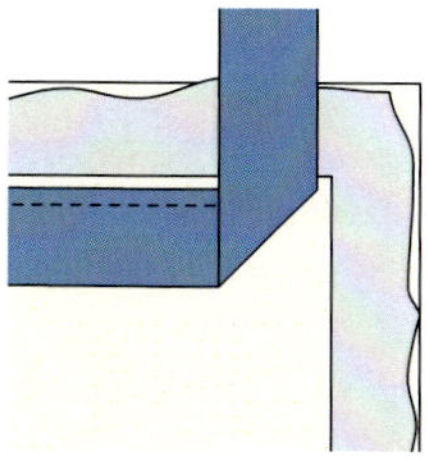

Fig. 43

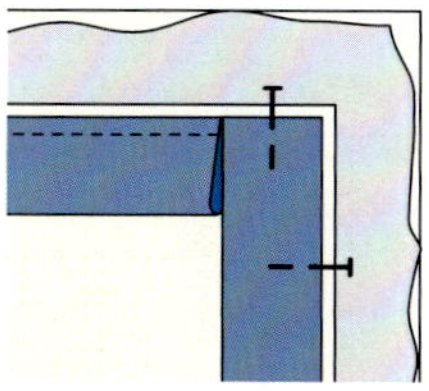

6. Backstitching at edge of quilt top, sew pinned binding to quilt (**Fig. 44**); backstitch when you reach the next mark. Lift needle out of fabric and clip thread.

Fig. 44

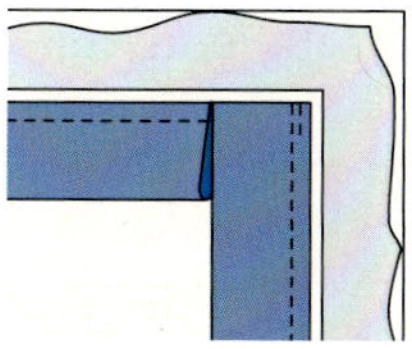

7. Repeat Steps 5 and 6 to continue sewing binding to quilt until binding overlaps beginning end by approximately 2". Trim excess binding.
8. If using $2^1/_2$"w binding (finished size $^1/_2$"), trim backing and batting a scant $^1/_4$" larger than quilt top so that batting and backing will fill the binding when it is folded over to the quilt backing. If using a different width binding, trim backing and batting according to project instructions.
9. On 1 edge of quilt, fold binding over to quilt backing and pin pressed edge in place, covering stitching line (**Fig. 45**). On adjacent side, fold binding over, forming a mitered corner (**Fig. 46**). Repeat to pin remainder of binding in place.

Fig. 45

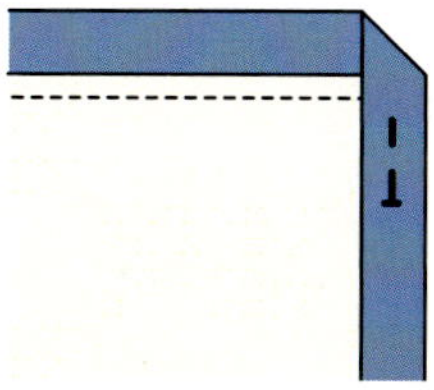

Fig. 46

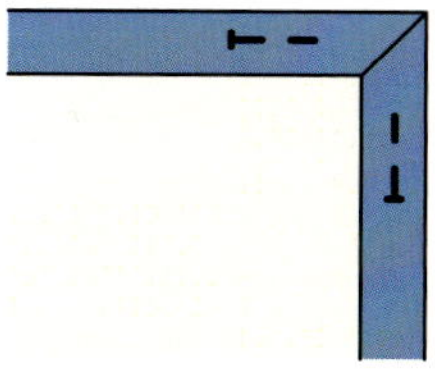

10. Blindstitch binding to backing, taking care not to stitch through to front of quilt.

ATTACHING BINDING WITH OVERLAPPED CORNERS

1. Matching raw edges and using a $^1/_4$" seam allowance, sew a length of binding to top and bottom edges on right side of quilt.
2. If using $2^1/_2$"w binding (finished size $^1/_2$"), trim backing and batting from top and bottom edges a scant $^1/_4$" larger than quilt top so that batting and backing will fill the binding when it is folded over to the quilt backing. If using different width binding, trim backing and batting even with edges of quilt top.
3. Trim ends of top and bottom binding even with edges of quilt top. Fold binding over to quilt backing and pin pressed edges in place, covering stitching line (**Fig. 47**); blindstitch binding to backing.

Fig. 47

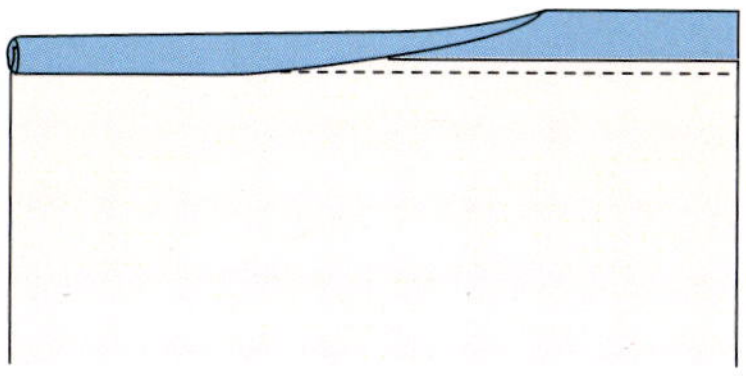

4. Leaving approximately $1^1/_2$" of binding at each end, stitch a length of binding to each side edge of quilt. Trim backing and batting as in Step 2.
5. Trim each end of binding $^1/_2$" longer than bound edge. Fold each end of binding over to quilt backing (**Fig. 48**); pin in place. Fold binding over to quilt backing and blindstitch in place, taking care not to stitch through to front of quilt.

Fig. 48

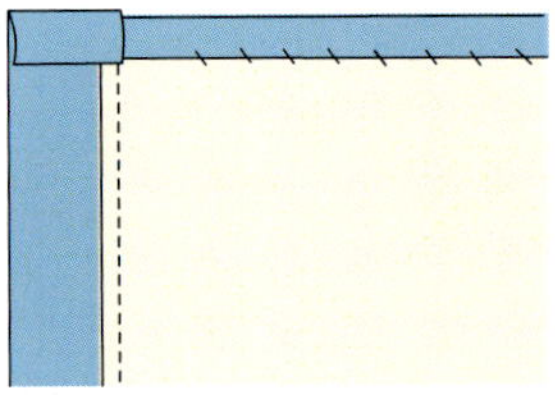

SIGNING AND DATING YOUR QUILT

Your completed quilt is a work of art and should be treated as such. And like any artist, you should sign and date your work. There are many different ways to do this, and you should pick a method of signing and dating that reflects the style of the quilt, the occasion for which it was made, and your own particular talents.

The following suggestions may give you an idea for recording the history of your quilt for future generations.

- Embroider your name, the date, and any additional information on the quilt top or backing. You may choose floss colors that closely match the fabric you are working on, such as white floss on a white border, or contrasting colors may be used.
- Make a label from muslin and use a permanent marker to write your information. Your label may be as plain or as fancy as you wish. Then stitch the label to the back of the quilt.
- Chart a cross-stitch label design that includes the information you wish and stitch it in colors that complement the quilt. Stitch the finished label to the quilt backing.

STENCILING

1. To make stencil, use a permanent marker to trace pattern onto plastic template material; cut out design with craft knife.
2. Place stencil in position on right side of fabric. Dip brush in paint and remove excess on paper towel. Brush should be almost dry. Apply paint in a stamping motion to fill in design area. Carefully remove stencil and allow to dry. Reposition stencil as necessary to complete stenciling.

Made in U.S.A.